Front cover: Part of a skirt border. Crete. See fig. 129

Frontispiece: Part of a cushion cover. Northern Sporades, Skyros. Silk on linen, double darning, satin, chain and stem stitches. Blue, red, green, yellow, white, brown, pink and black. Length 85.8 cm. Width 29.9 cm. Dawkins Collection. T.61-1950

Victoria & Albert Museum

A GUIDE TO GREEK ISLAND EMBROIDERY

Pauline Johnstone

London   1972

ISBN 0-905209-13-3

CONTENTS

4 *Acknowledgments*

5 *Introduction*
5 Collectors and sources
6 Uses of embroidery
6 Patterns and history
8 Island conditions
8 The raw materials
9 Dating

10 *The Dodecanese*
10 The bed tent
11 Rhodes
11 Cos
11 Symi
12 Nisyros
12 Tilos
12 Kalymnos
13 Karpathos
13 Patmos
14 Astypalaia

16 *The Cyclades*
17 Amorgos
18 Milos
18 Pholegandros
18 Siphnos
18 Naxos
19 Anaphi
19 Ios
20 Mykonos
20 Kimolos

21 *The Northern Islands*
21 The Northern Sporades
21 Thasos
21 Chios
22 Mytilini
22 Samos

23 *Epirus and the Ionian Islands*

26 *The Greek Mainland*

28 *Crete*

31 *Cyprus*

32 *Bibliography*

Plates

Map

Acknowledgments

I have been greatly helped in the preparation of this study by many friends who have given generously of their time and knowledge. I am particularly grateful to Mr Donald King, Keeper, Department of Textiles, for his valuable comments on the text, and to the staff of this Department, now my colleagues, who were consistently helpful to an outsider working among them; to the Worshipful Company of Weavers, whose generosity enabled me to visit Greece; to Miss Priscilla Boys-Smith for allowing me to study her collection. I should also like to thank Mrs H. Polychroniadis of the Benaki Museum, Athens; Mrs P. Zora of the Museum of Popular Art, Athens; Mrs T. Oikonomidis; Dr Frank Walton, Director of the Gennadius Library, Athens, and his staff; Dr E. Borboudakis of the Archaeological Museum, Iraklion; Dr Parlamas, Director of the Society of Cretan Studies, Iraklion; Professor N. V. Drandakis and Miss T. Lina of the University of Joannina; Mrs A. Peiridhou of the Archaeological Museum, Nicosia; and Professor M. Manoussacas, Director of the Hellenic Institute, Venice, for his most helpful bibliographical indications.
P.J.

INTRODUCTION

Collectors and sources

The large collections of embroidery from the Greek islands in this country, mostly now in museums, owe their existence to the interest and appreciation of English visitors to Greece at the end of the last and the beginning of this century.[1]

At that time embroidery as a domestic art had already virtually died out in most of the islands, and even these early collectors were too late to obtain first-hand information. Nevertheless, it is on their indications and researches, tentative as they necessarily were, that present-day knowledge of the subject largely rests. At present we know of very few written records, such as wills and marriage contracts, which have any relevance. Another difficulty is that intermarriage and travel among the islands caused the movement of household chattels as well as of people, and the fact that any one embroidery was acquired in a given island is not necessarily proof that it was made there. The point is well illustrated by an incident related by Robert Pashley in his *Travels in Crete*: 'During the evening our host and his wife were visited by an elderly dame, accompanied by her young and beautiful daughter, whose dress, peculiar to one of the islands of the Archipelago, struck me, on account of the great difference between it and that of every other woman in Crete. I learnt that she is a native of this village, but having fled to the islands, with thousands of her sex, for protection and security, during the continuance of the war in Crete, she had not yet abandoned, since her return, the costume of her place of refuge.'[2]

The earliest of the English collectors was Thomas Sandwith, British Consul in Crete from 1870 to 1885, whose Cretan embroideries and laces were acquired by the Victoria and Albert Museum in 1876. Unfortunately no local information was supplied at the time. Another was Theodore Bent, who travelled in the islands in 1883-4. Three very fine dresses from Karpathos now in the Museum collection were brought back by him [25-26].

In the earliest years of this century a group of scholars at the British School of Archaeology in Athens, including the Director of the time, Professor Carr Bosanquet, began to take an interest in the embroideries. Among them were R. M. Dawkins and A. J. B. Wace,[3] who treated the subject as a serious study and amassed rich collections, both from travel in the islands and through dealers in Athens, Istanbul and Smyrna. The information which they collected in the islands at this time provides in many cases the most reliable guidance available for the attribution of these embroideries, and it is due to their efforts that this information has been preserved. Their findings were condensed in the catalogue of an exhibition of Greek Island embroideries held by the Burlington Fine Arts Club in 1914, which included some of their own pieces and those of their fellow enthusiasts connected with the British School in Athens, Guy Dickens, A. M. Daniel and Miss Louisa Pesel. Other collections made at this period were those of Sir Arthur Church, P. E. Newberry and Mrs F. H. Cook. This latter is the subject of Wace's best known work in this field.[4]

About two-thirds of the large number of embroideries now in the Victoria and Albert Museum, which form the subject of this study, is made up of the complete Dawkins collection, which he gave to the Museum in 1950. With it is a manuscript catalogue kept at the time the collection was made, but this is unfortunately incomplete and the numbers in it do not tally with those on the embroideries. It is therefore by no means possible to identify all the pieces referred to in the catalogue, but in certain instances it provides valuable clues as to origin.

Apart from the researches of Wace and Dawkins, the Greek authority Angeliki Hadjimichaeli, who died in 1965, had a very wide personal knowledge of the islands and their folk art, particularly the embroideries, and her published work is of great value. The work of the Greek costume illustrator, Athena Tarsouli, also throws some light on the embroideries. The finest Greek collections are in the Benaki Museum and the Museum of Popular Art in Athens.

A certain amount of work on this subject was also done during the period of Italian jurisdiction in the Dodecanese by Marica Montesanto.

For information contemporary with the embroideries the researcher can turn to the European travellers who visited the islands and published accounts of their

[1] The principal collections in the United Kingdom, apart from the Victoria and Albert Museum, are in the Royal Scottish Museum, Edinburgh, the City of Liverpool Museums, the Fitzwilliam Museum, Cambridge, the Whitworth Art Gallery, Manchester, and the Ashmolean Museum, Oxford.
[2] R. Pashley, *Travels in Crete*, vol. II, 1837, p. 109. At the time of Pashley's visit in 1834 the Cyclades were already part of the Kingdom of Greece, while Crete was still under Moslem rule.
[3] R. M. Dawkins became Director of the British School at Athens 1906-14 and Professor of Byzantine and Modern Greek Language and Literature at Oxford 1920-39. A. J. B. Wace was Director of the British School at Athens 1914-23, Keeper of Textiles in the Victoria and Albert Museum 1924-34, Professor of Classical Archaeology, Cambridge, 1934-44, Professor of Classics and Archaeology, Farouk I University, Alexandria, 1943-52, Member of the Institute of Advanced Study, Princeton, etc.
[4] *Mediterranean and Near Eastern embroideries from the collection of Mrs F. H. Cook*, 1935.

5

voyages, from Cristoforo Buondelmonti in 1422 to the end of the nineteenth century. Their descriptions, however, tend to be brief, and when not concerned with actual details of travel, are almost invariably geographical or, in the case of later writers, archaeological. The most helpful are probably the two French botanists, Pierre Belon and Joseph Pitton de Tournefort, who travelled in the Levant in the middle of the sixteenth century and 1700 respectively.[5] Even Tournefort, who observed and illustrated with care the costume of the islands, does not reproduce embroidery patterns which correspond to any actual garment. In the works of many other travellers who described visits to the islands only the most casual passing references to embroidery can be found, although their comments on conditions and life in the islands can be revealing. The Englishman Theodore Bent, who has already been mentioned, was sufficiently interested in the subject to describe embroidery wherever he saw it, but it is clear that at the time of his voyage in the Cyclades in 1883 home-made embroidery had been largely superseded by imported brocades.[6]

Uses of embroidery

Traditionally, in Greece and the Greek islands, it was expected that a girl's dowry would include a number of embroidered dresses and household articles, most of which she had worked herself, and these would figure in her marriage contract. Household embroideries consisted mainly of furnishings for the marriage bed, which were used for display at the wedding and on festival occasions thereafter. They naturally differed in different regions to suit local architectural and domestic traditions.

In the Dodecanese and southern Cyclades, the bed was a raised platform or alcove in the single living room, which might be compared to the box-bed of the Scottish highland croft, rather than a bedstead. In these regions privacy was ensured by an enclosing tent, or by curtains, while the edge of the platform was decorated with a valance. (The Greeks used the Italian name *mostra:* a display.) Elsewhere ordinary bedspreads were used, embroidered on all four borders. Everywhere the bed was piled with a number of cushions or pillows in embroidered covers, and in some houses long cushions would be used on the Turkish-style divan in the living room.

Coloured silk embroidery on dress was normally on the white linen under-dress, most of which would be invisible beneath an outer dress of coloured silk or cotton. Styles differed from island to island, and embroidery on the under-dress was placed where it would show, according to the cut of the outer dress. In practice this was usually at neck, wrists and hem, unless the over-dress was sleeveless, when the whole sleeve of the under-dress would be embroidered (for example in Tilos and Astypalaia, figs. 22, 34).

The importance of the embroideries in domestic life is shown by mention of them in traditional songs and in stories which were handed down almost verbatim. It is assumed that in most cases girls learned to embroider at home, but a story from Cos shows that this was not always so. The same story gives a list of embroidered articles which corresponds exactly to existing pieces: 'Once there was an embroideress who took pupils, and she used to teach them to embroider shifts, napkins, face-cloths, veils, kerchiefs, bed-tents and their doors, sheets, pillow-cases and all sorts of cloth furnishings.'[7] This suggests that not all embroideries were worked by girls for their own use, but that the professional worker also existed. We know from Belon's account of the Dodecanese (see p. 10) that embroidery could be bought there in the sixteenth century, and some of the larger embroideries, for example bed tents and curtains such as those shown at figs. 1, 10 and 52, could well have been professional work.

Patterns and history

The patterns used in these embroideries were not, as far as we can tell, greatly subject to changes in fashion. Once a traditional design became established in a certain island, it appears to have been repeated almost stitch for stitch by succeeding generations. The island girl's deeply rooted acceptance of tradition is illustrated by the reply given to the French writer Savary, who took the women of Kimolos to task for what he regarded as the ugliness of their dress: 'Our grandmothers were clad in the same way; we do but follow the custom.'[8]

The island patterns are highly distinctive, but the history of the area can be traced in the individual motifs which form the basis of the patterns. In many cases similar motifs have been worked into a completely different synthesis in different island groups.

All the islands of the Aegean and Ionian seas formed part of the Byzantine Empire until late in the twelfth century. During the late medieval period, however, and particularly after the sack of Constantinople in 1204, almost all were in Frankish hands. Most of the island overlords of this time were of Italian origin, Roman, Neapolitan, Sicilian, Genoese and above all Venetian, and it was Venice which in the end ruled almost exclusively in the Ionian islands, the Cyclades, Cyprus and Crete. The fifteenth and sixteenth centuries, on the other hand, saw constant pressure from the rising Turkish empire, especially after the fall of Constantinople in 1453, and by the middle of the sixteenth century most of the Aegean was under Turkish jurisdiction. Only Crete remained Venetian until 1669.

Three main periods therefore, the Byzantine, the Venetian and the Turkish, had their influence on island life, and to a certain extent each is reflected in the embroidery patterns. Many of the patterns are based on stylized plant forms, which is usual in all peasant embroidery, but formal bird and animal motifs, peacocks, parrots, eagles, stags, etc., held a particular place in the Greek islands. Stylized animal decoration, particularly the so-called Tree of Life design, where two animals or birds are confronted across a tree or plant [36, 105], spread from Central Asia throughout the Middle East, and became a classic pattern in silks from Byzantine workshops. It remained current in all Mediterranean countries over a very long period, and was widely reproduced in peasant and household embroideries. As Wace has pointed out, it is impossible to tell whether this type of decoration came to the Greek islands as part of a general Mediterranean heritage passed on through Byzantium, or as a more direct influence from Italian models,[9] but in view of the popularity of this type of pattern in Italian household weaving and embroidery in the fifteenth and sixteenth centuries, and the role played by the Italians in the islands at this period, the latter explanation seems more likely. One motif widely used in the island embroideries, the double-headed eagle [63], was certainly inherited from Byzantium and used as a patriotic symbol after the fall of Constantinople, and the popularity of the peacock may also be traceable to Byzantine origins [70, 105].

Floral patterns in the Turkish manner were taken from pottery design, especially in the Northern Sporades [82], and more directly from Turkish embroidery, which supplied the characteristic rose and cypress motifs. Some headscarves, in particular, are very close indeed to Turkish models.

In a slightly different sense the influence of Italian and Turkish silk textiles can also be seen. Wace's theory[10] that the embroideries were originally inspired by a desire to emulate the valuable silks which were priced far above the means of the country people is borne out by an unfinished fragment of Naxos embroidery from the Dawkins collection [62], which shows clearly the relationship between the pattern and a standard type of Turkish silk design.[11] In general, however, there was no attempt to copy silk patterns with any exactitude, but rather to take certain features and repeat them in a way which suggests the recurring patterns of fabrics woven on a loom [33]. Derivation from silk patterns shows more clearly in some of the embroideries than in others. For example, Turkish embroidered bedspreads from Asia Minor appear to have been copied directly from silks. Embroideries from Epirus using the same technique and in much the same style are in some ways very close to the Turkish examples but they have departed farther from the original silk designs. Indeed it is a feature of many of these Epirote embroideries that the designs are not repetitive.[12] Again, one of the two traditional versions of the famous Cretan skirt pattern [123] suggests very strongly the repeating design of a certain type of Italian silk of the seventeenth century, while the other is a frieze based on a formal vase of carnations [121], which was another motif popular in Italian silks of the same period. It has also been suggested that the single motifs which occur frequently in embroideries from the Dodecanese [2] could be compared to the huge isolated pomegranate patterns from Turkish silks, particularly those made for the sultan's robes in the fifteenth century.[13] This argument, however, is rather hard to follow, and if the Dodecanesian embroideries can be said to have derived from Turkish silk patterns at all, it seems more likely that the comparison should be made with the stylized repeating leaf/flower patterns from Patmian curtains and the door panels of Rhodian and Coan bed tents [33, 1].

[5]P. Belon du Mans, *Les observations de plusieurs singularitez et choses mémorables*, 1553. J. Pitton de Tournefort, *Relation d'un voyage du Levant*, 1717, Eng. trs. *A voyage into the Levant*, 1718.

[6]J. T. Bent, *The Cyclades*, 1885, reprinted Chicago, 1966.

[7]R. M. Dawkins, *Forty-five stories from the Dodecanese*, 1950, p. 369.

[8]C. E. Savary (Eng. trs.), *Letters on Greece*, 1788, p. 399.

[9]*Burlington Fine Arts Club Catalogue*, 1914, p. xxix.

[10]A. J. B. Wace, in the introduction to Tahsin Öz, *Turkish textiles and velvets*, 1950, pp. x-xi.

[11]See under Naxos, p. 18.

[12]Illustrations of embroideries from Asia Minor, in Wace, *Med. and N.E. embroideries*, pls. CVII-CXXI, show very clearly the close relationship with Turkish silks. Certain motifs in the Epirote embroideries (for example Wace, pl. xii of T.216-1920 and T.249-1950 [96]) have similar characteristics but are less formally presented. The flower motifs may be compared with Turkish silks illustrated by Tahsin Öz, *Turkish textiles and velvets*, pls. XXIX and XXXIV.

[13]A. J. B. Wace in the introduction to Tahsin Öz, *ibid*.

7

Island conditions

Embroideries are in fact attributed to a relatively small number of islands, particularly among the Cyclades, where it would seem that in very many of the islands no embroidery was made at all. It is possible that existing attributions are made on insufficient information and that they should be extended to cover a greater number of islands, but if it is in fact the case that some islands embroidered while others did not, the factors which governed this situation seem impossible to define.

Conditions of life in the Aegean between the fourteenth and eighteenth centuries were hazardous in the extreme. War between Byzantium and the Frankish overlords, between the Franks themselves, above all between Venice and Turkey, remained a constant background. Indeed the naval war between Muslim and Christian developed from sporadic operations by privateers on either side to out-and-out piracy for private gain, which terrorized the eastern Mediterranean into the nineteenth century. To this were added the hazards of plague, famine, and in some cases purely geographical disadvantage, and these causes could wipe out entire populations, remove every able-bodied male in a community to slavery under the Turks, or result in wholesale emigration. These disasters, however, alternated at different times and in different islands with periods of considerable prosperity, and in general trade in various natural products, notably olive oil, corn and cotton, was at all times fairly lively. (It is interesting that a French ambassador to the Sultan in the early seventeenth century, speaking with particular reference to Castelorizo, remarks that the inhabitants of fertile islands tilled their soil and remained poor, while those who were forced to turn to their ships for a livelihood traded and grew rich.[14] This was also true of Patmos.)

Nevertheless it is difficult to form a coherent picture of the relationship between these factors and an embroidery tradition. Large and generally prosperous islands like Rhodes, Cos and Naxos had embroidery, others such as Andros and Syros did not; the remote, poor island Anaphi apparently produced an enormous amount, while its more fertile neighbour Thira seems to have made none.[15]

The raw materials

It has generally been assumed[16] that it was the availability of the raw materials, flax, cotton and in particular silk, that made it possible for the women of these frequently impoverished communities to produce such luxurious articles, but in fact it would seem that cotton was the only one of the three that was freely available in virtually every island. Cotton figures prominently in seventeenth and eighteenth century lists of island products, while cotton spinning, and above all the knitting of cotton stockings, are referred to constantly by travellers who never mention embroidery.[17]

Only the Ionian islands are mentioned as producers of flax. Marseilles imported it from them in the seventeenth century, and travellers early in the nineteenth list it among the products of Ithaka and Kythera.[18] Yet many embroideries from the Aegean were worked on linen. In fact both cotton and linen were used as ground materials, and also mixtures of the two, but here again no specific picture emerges, unless it could be said, in very general terms, that apparently the older embroideries are more often worked on linen. It is only in Crete that the use of a linen/cotton mixture can be described as a definite characteristic.

It is equally difficult to relate the production of embroidery in one island or another to the production of raw silk. It is noticeable that very few islands are mentioned as producers of silk, and that it is precisely these, Andros, Tinos, Kythnos and Kea, among others, that appear to have no tradition of embroidery. The exceptions are Naxos, Crete and Cyprus, all of which were silk producers and also embroidered, and to a lesser extent Chios, which produced and imported silk for its own weaving industry and also made a very few embroideries, and Siphnos, which is said by Tournefort to have produced a small amount of fine quality silk.[19]

It is perhaps possible that islands producing enough silk to make export[20] worthwhile gave it all to this end, while in others a handful of silkworms reared on the occasional mulberry tree produced only enough for home needs, but it seems equally likely that islands with no silk of their own imported enough for their embroidery from their silk-producing neighbours, or from the mainland silk-producing districts such as the Peloponnese, Thessaly and Asia Minor.

The decline of embroidery as a household art during the nineteenth century, which seems to have been virtually complete in the islands if not on the mainland, has been linked with the fall in silk production, caused by the dying out of the silk

[14]Des Hayes, *Voiage de Leuant*, 1624, p. 323, 'Parce que leur terroir est fort sterile, ils s'addonnent à la navigation, qui les enrichit tellement, qu'il n'y en a point qui ne soient à leur aise, et qui n'ayent des vaisseaux.'

[15]The Dawkins manuscript catalogue suggests 'Milos or Thira' for certain pieces (nos. 119, 487, 514) but this attribution must be regarded as very tentative.

[16]Wace, *Med. and N. E. embroideries*, p. 15.

[17]In 1700 Tournefort mentioned cotton in several islands and spoke of an abundance in Thira, where, he said, nuns made 'the best Calicoes in the Country; they are carry'd to Candia, the Morea, and to all parts of the Archipelago' (*A voyage into the Levant*, vol. I, p. 209). Ios and Mykonos are mentioned by Pasch di Krienen as producers of knitted caps and stockings (*Breve descrizione dell'Arcipelago*, 1771, pp. 32 and 83). The German archaeologist Ludwig Ross mentioned the knitting of cotton stockings as the most important industry in the island of Patmos. Formerly the women spun the yarn themselves, but by 1841 it was imported from England and they confined themselves to knitting. (*Reisen auf den griechischen Inseln*, 1840-45, vol. II, p. 133.)

weaving industry in Chios and Bursa after the introduction of the power loom in western Europe enabled cheap European silks to capture the Turkish market.[21] At the same period the Greek War of Independence, resulting in the creation of the Kingdom of Greece in 1832, severed contacts between the Cyclades and the Turkish silk markets. Silk, however, continued to be produced and to some extent manufactured in Greece (principally in Kalamata) in the nineteenth century, while the silk producing industry of Anatolia increased greatly in order to meet the demands of the European power looms. It seems therefore that silk for embroidery must have been available in the area as a whole, had the islanders wanted it. A more likely explanation is that they preferred the manufactured silks to the hand-made substitutes, as soon as these could be obtained at a more reasonable price, and this is borne out by Bent's descriptions of island costume in the 1880s, which refer to silk dresses but never to embroidery.

Dating

The question of dating any of these embroideries has been summed up by Wace, who said, 'It is impossible to assign with any degree of certainty a date to any piece of Greek embroidery, unless it happens to have the date worked on it,'[22] and this statement remains equally true today. It is evident from the poem of Georgillas and from Belon's remarks on bed tents (p. 10) that embroidery was made in the Dodecanese in the late fifteenth and sixteenth centuries, but no existing piece could with certainty be given such an early date. In most cases the seventeenth or more often the eighteenth century seems more likely.

The only known embroideries which are actually dated are Cretan skirts. The earliest known is a fragment in the Metropolitan Museum, New York, dated 1697, while others date from the first half of the eighteenth century.[23] Bent, who travelled in the islands in the 1880s, said that the dresses he brought home from Karpathos had not been worn for a hundred and fifty years. Other than this, there is no direct evidence.

It is possible that conditions in the islands should again be taken into account in this connexion. It does appear from the descriptions of travellers that many islands were reduced to extreme poverty in the eighteenth century, while on the other hand some at least knew greater prosperity during the seventeenth: Patmos and Milos are cases in point. Since it seems on the face of it more likely that elaborate embroideries for the marriage bed would be made in conditions of affluence rather than of near destitution, it is possible that some of the finer bed hangings should be dated to the seventeenth century rather than later. For the rest the traditional patterns were followed very closely, probably over long periods, and therefore there seems to be no means of telling when any of these embroideries were made. The traditional attribution to the eighteenth century is in fact no more than guesswork.

[18]Masson, *Histoire de commerce français dans le Levant au XVIIme siècle*, 1896, p. 440; H. W. Williams, *Travels in Italy and Greece*, 1820, App. II; H. Holland, *Travels in the Ionian Islands*, 2nd ed., 1819, p. 62.

[19]*A voyage into the Levant*, vol. I, p. 135.

[20]Chios imported silk for its weaving industry from neighbouring islands, notably Tinos, Andros and Mytilini (Argenti, *The costumes of Chios*, 1953, p. 45). Some would certainly have gone to the Turkish silk weavers, probably via Smyrna. Around 1700 Marseilles was importing 70,000 lbs. of silk annually from the islands. That of Tinos was especially sought after, and the inhabitants took it to Smyrna themselves to sell to the French. Island silk was considered particularly suitable for thread and ribbons. Imports to France went to Tours for the ribbon manufacturers (R. Paris, *Histoire du commerce de Marseille*, vol. V, 1959, p. 474. Masson, *op. cit.* pp. 428, 508.) Silk was used in the islands for the knitting of stockings (Tinos) and for handwoven dresses and scarves.

[21]Wace, *Burlington Fine Arts Club Catalogue*, 1914, p. vii.

[22]Wace, *ibid.*, p. xxiv.

[23]*Metropolitan Museum of Art Bulletin*, April 1943, p. 254. There is another border dated 1726 in the Metropolitan Museum, and three in the Victoria and Albert Museum, 2054-1876, T.97-1967 and 2051-1876, dated 1733, 1757 and 1762 respectively.

THE DODECANESE

The town of Rhodes was captured by the Knights of St John from the Byzantines in 1309, and thereafter most of the twelve islands were ruled by them until they los. Rhodes to the Turks in 1523. In fact their presence appears to have had a merely negative effect on embroidery design, in that the strong Italian influence which can be seen in island groups which were mainly under Venetian suzerainty is noticeably lacking in the Dodecanese, and this is readily understandable, since the Knights were of many nationalities and were in any case a near-monastic order whose presence would obviously have made less impression on the domestic arts than that of rulers who brought their families and the elaborate entourage of a feudal lord to their new domains.

One characteristic of Dodecanesian embroidery was the use of large isolated motifs, which differed in design and also had different names in different islands. In Rhodes they were called 'glastra' (lit. a flower pot), and Wace uses this name throughout his writings. Dawkins, in his manuscript catalogue, describes them simply as 'blobs'. Some types of glastra suggest a compact variation of the Tree of Life pattern. Elsewhere the 'blob' may be in the form of a star, or just an abstract pattern [23, 24].

Another device common to Rhodes, Cos and Patmos was a pair of leaves surmounted by a complicated three-pronged pattern of birds, trees and miniature flowers which must originally have derived from a flower shape [33]. In this form it is found only in the Dodecanese, but both leaves and 'flower' were used separately in the Dodecanese and southern Cyclades [44, 54]. For easy reference Wace christened the leaf motif the King Pattern and the flower the Queen. The combination of leaves and flower, King and Queen, can be seen at its clearest on the bed tents of Cos [10], in a compressed form on Rhodian tents [3] and as a repeating pattern on the curtains of Patmos [33]. The Greek name for the leaf pattern is *platyphylla* - the broad leaves.

The bed tent

The marriage bed tent was a feature peculiar to the Dodecanese, where the style of domestic architecture produced a square bed platform set in a corner of the room, which demanded a bed tent to provide privacy rather than a simple curtain. These tents, or sparvers, carry some of the best embroidery of the islands. The only surviving examples are attributed to Rhodes and Cos [1, 10], but it is certain that they were used in Tilos since they are mentioned in one of the songs of the island, and perhaps in other islands as well.[24] Dawkins notes in his manuscript catalogue that he saw a bed tent from Tilos in the house of a doctor in Nisyros.

Bed tents were evidently known in this area since medieval times. Wace mentions one shown in a twelfth century fresco in Cyprus.[25] It is not known when they were first embroidered, but embroidery on sparvers and other household articles figures in a Rhodian poet's description of the activities of the ladies of the town in the last years of the fifteenth century.[26] In the middle of the sixteenth century the French botanist Pierre Belon du Mans says of Rhodes: 'Lon y trouve à acheter de beaux ouvrages de soie faictz à l'aiguille, et principalement des pavillons de licts. Ilz font leurs ouvrages de diverses couleurs, en maniere de poincts croisez. Le portraict est de feuillages, et est different à l'ouvrage Turquois, et à celuy qui est faict à Chio et en Cypre.'[27]

The tents consisted of tapering strips of linen joined to a wooden ring at the top to form a bell tent. The front was heavily embroidered with glastra devices and borders of leaves or stars on each strip, while the back had less decoration or none at all. The most elaborate examples had an opening in the front set in a special door panel, on which some particularly fine embroidery was worked, especially on the gable over the opening [1, 10].

Two distinct types of embroidery are found in the Dodecanese which are quite different in effect, although patterns, colours and stitches are on analysis very similar. Both used cross stitch, mainly in red and green, but in one case the stitches and the linen on which they were worked were fine [13], and much embroidery was also worked in fine pattern darning. In the second type by contrast the linen was heavy and the stitches close and thick in texture. Cross stitch was worked in a

[24]Wace, *Med. and N. E. embroideries*, p. 23. Montesanto, *L'Isola dei Gigli*, 1932, p. 40, mentions them in Astypalaia.
[25]Wace, *loc. cit.*
[26]The poem is the θανατικὸν τῆς Ρόδου, a lament for Rhodes after an outbreak of plague, written by a native of the town, Emmanuel Georgillas, in 1498 (published W. Wagner, *Carmina Graeca Medii Aevi*, 1874, II.170 ff. for the reference to embroidery). The word used for bed tent is παρμπέρη instead of the more usual σπερβέρη. He praises the skill of the girls and lists the flowers and vines (including the 'broad leaf') which they work into their embroideries.
[27]Belon, *Les observations de plusieurs singularitez*, vol. II, 1553, p. 90.
[28]Other stitches found in the Dodecanese include raised cross stitch, double running in steps, long-armed cross and threaded stitches worked on a ground of running stitches.

thick loosely twisted silk which produced a highly individual curly effect [3]. All authorities agree in attributing bed furnishings of this second type to Rhodes and, although there appears to be no documented example to support the theory, the tradition is very strong and there is equally no reason to disagree with it. Apart from the use of twisted silk, various other techniques were employed in the southern islands, especially Karpathos and Astypalaia [28, 34], to produce a thick appearance.[28]

Rhodes In Rhodes the large village of Lindos, which was the site of a classical temple and of a crusading fortress, and in the seventeenth century a flourishing port, was an important centre for embroidery, and in particular for the famous sparvers.[29] (It must be remembered that during the period of Turkish rule the Greek population was not permitted to live in the town of Rhodes itself but only in the suburbs and villages.) Apart from the bed tents, deep valances made of three loom widths of linen joined horizontally were decorated with large glastra patterns and leaves [4, 6] and sometimes with ewers [5]. (The long-spouted ewer looks like a coffee pot to western eyes, but would have been used for water.) Cushion covers were also decorated with King pattern leaves arranged separately in rows, and often with a cross device in the centre [7, 8].

The short full skirt of the Rhodian under-dress in the collection [9] cleared the tops of the knee-high leather leggings which were part of the costume of the island, while the band of embroidery on the hem showed below the pleated overskirt.[30]

Cos The finer type of embroidery (in particular the bed tents and valances comparable to them) is generally attributed to Cos on the evidence of the bed tent which formerly belonged to the Platanistas family of Cos [10-12]. This piece illustrates admirably the type of door gable associated with the lighter type of embroidery. It was acquired from an Englishman, W. R. Paton, who lived in Kalymnos at the end of the last century and obtained the bed tent from the Platanistas family. According to a letter written by him at the time (1902), 'These particular kind of bed hangings, and the style of the work, are strictly confined to a certain group of islands, Cos, Calymnos, Astypalaia, Lipsos (possibly Leros and Patmos).' We have already seen that bed tents were made in Tilos, and it is possible that they were of the same type, although Dawkins likens the one he saw to both the Rhodian and the Coan varieties. A panel from a bed tent of the Coan type in the Ashmolean Museum is ascribed to Leros, and another from a curtain in a quite different style to Kalymnos (p. 20 and fig. 74).[31]

Valances in the finer technique are very similar in style to the Rhodian examples [14], but usually have their own characteristic glastra patterns. Most of the cushion covers attributed to Cos [16-18] depart from the bed tent and valance designs except for the so-called lady-in-castle pattern, which was often used in the gables of bed tents. A cushion (T.549-1950) which substitutes a parrot in a cage for the lady was acquired by Dawkins in Leros and bears out the assumption that the embroideries of this group of islands were similar.

Symi After Rhodes and Cos, Symi was one of the most important islands of the Dodecanese. It was renowned as a centre of ship building, and was the chief of the sponge-fishing islands, being joined in this trade by Kalymnos and Khalki at a relatively recent date. The island surrendered voluntarily to the Turks after the fall of Rhodes in 1523, and obtained important privileges from the Sultan, which became the model for Turkish treatment of the rest of the Dodecanese, apart from Rhodes and Cos. Hence the name the Privileged Islands. It was also, with Patmos, an important centre of Greek education in the eighteenth century.

This history suggests that it is very difficult to relate a rich tradition of embroidery to either prosperity or poverty in any given island. If it is assumed that it was the relative prosperity and higher standard of living of Rhodes, Cos and Patmos which led to the decoration of the islanders' houses with fine embroideries, Symi could have been expected to follow suit. In fact we have very few indications of embroidery made in Symi. A valance bought there by Dawkins (T.367-1950) is very similar to the valance T.375-1950 [15].

[29]Montesanto, *La città sacra, Lindo*, 1932, p. 53. Des Hayes, *Voiage du Leuant*, 1624, p. 321, says, 'Le bourg de Lindo, qui est situé du costé de Siroc, est aussi tout habité de Chrestiens, qui sont fort riches, à cause du trafic qu'ils font avec leurs vaisseaux qui sont les plus beaux de Turquie.'
[30]For illustrations of Rhodian costume see Tarsouli, *Embroideries and costumes of the Dodecanese*, 1951, pls. 1-3, 8-10.
[31]Ashmolean Museum, Lady Myres Bequest, nos. 1960-115 and 1960-120. The embroideries belonged to the archaeologist Sir John Myres.

Nisyros This island was known to Pliny and also in the Byzantine period as a source of shells for the making of purple dye, the colour which was so admired and sought after by the Byzantines for the dyeing of silks from the imperial workrooms. It is possible that these same shells, less expertly used, account for the pinky-purplish colouring in two attractive valances from Nisyros, which have the island's characteristic small glastra device in the centre and a border of tiny human figures [19]. A more usual colour scheme in the island, uncommon elsewhere, was a combination of light blue, yellow and brown, which is found in valances and cushion covers [20].

Tilos Two types of under-dress prevailed in the costume of the Dodecanese, one with a full skirt gathered at the waist, the other, evidently of much older design probably dating from the Byzantine period, a straight shift with wide straight sleeves. The Rhodian dress [9] mentioned above belongs to the first type. The islands of Nisyros, Tilos and Astypalaia have not only full skirts but also long full sleeves gathered at the top on to a dropped shoulder seam. This sleeve is revealed by the sleeveless over-dress, and is heavily embroidered in vertical stripes which differ in the three islands.[32] The collection lacks such a dress from Nisyros, where the sleeve pattern was called 'the little fishes' and the embroidery was often worked in brown, as in the furnishings, but possesses three from Tilos, with characteristic green sleeve stripes in a pattern of flowerets [22]. The likelihood that bed tents were made in the island has already been discussed (p. 10). A large valance in the collection [23] compares to a similar piece attributed by Marica Montesanto to Tilos.[33] It is chiefly distinguishable from a Rhodian valance by the design of the glastra motif.

Kalymnos The shift type of under-dress is represented by Kalymnos and Karpathos, although the two are very different.

In Kalymnos the dresses are exquisitely worked in fine cross stitch, on linen woven with groups of cotton warp stripes [29, 30]. The main ornament is in medallions on the front of the skirt, but the dresses are meticulously finished, with a band of embroidery at the neck terminating in a small insertion of decorative open-work at the base of the neck-opening. Neck and sleeves are trimmed with a narrow multicoloured lace edging of the *bibila*[31] type and the tie strings at the neck are finished with *bibila* lace and minute tassels. The dress was worn under an over-dress of dark striped silk, open at the front and slit at the side seams. Decorum demanded that in church the front of the over-dress should be closed like a coat,

1. Costume of Karpathos. Reproduced from Stackelberg, Costumes et usages des peuples de la Grèce moderne, *1825.*

but after church one side of the skirt was tucked up to the waistband to reveal the embroidery on the under-dress.[35]

It has already been mentioned (p. 11) that a certain type of bed hanging may have come from Kalymnos [74]. In addition cotton valances, probably of nineteenth century date, with embroidery which resembles that on the dresses, are tentatively attributed to the island for that reason [31].

Karpathos Three dresses were brought back from Karpathos by Theodore Bent after his visit to the island in 1884, and were acquired by the Museum in 1886 [25, 26]. Bent had been told that they had not been worn for a hundred and fifty years. These are also of the straight type, but they are immensely long and have a deep tuck taken up across the skirt, so that the garment as it is worn has the appearance of a separate tunic and skirt. The embroidery, which is in the dark red and greens and heavy stitches typical of the Dodecanese, is arranged accordingly. They were clearly not intended to be worn under an outer dress. Two of these dresses are made of raw silk crepe, and it is assumed that some household embroideries from Karpathos which are made of this material are older than those worked on linen. Such a dress was illustrated by Baron Stackelberg [I] in the early years of the nineteenth century (that is, nearly a hundred years later than the date of the dresses in the Museum collection, if Bent's information is assumed to be accurate).[36] Stackelberg, however, attributed his sketch not to Karpathos but to Kasos. A traveller just before his time described the women's dress in Kasos and made it clear that the costume included an embroidered dress of fine cotton with a short sleeveless jacket and a sash.[37] There is no doubt that the Bent dresses represent the older form of costume from Karpathos. The importance attached to these magnificent garments as a significant part of a girl's dowry is shown by Bent's information that one of the dresses was a 'best' dress (that is, the one which was entered first in the marriage contract) and another was a 'second best' dress. At some time during the nineteenth century this older costume ceased to be worn in the island, and the later type of shift, which was worn in the usual way under an over-dress, had merely a narrow band of floral embroidery at the neck and down the front of the bodice.[38]

Patmos Two of the northernmost islands of the Dodecanese have embroidery which is much nearer that of the Cyclades, and for this reason they have been left till last. The embroideries of both are extremely interesting.

The monastery of St John the Divine on Patmos, founded in the eleventh century, saved the island from much of the war and violence which ravaged the Aegean in the Middle Ages, since the piety and learning of the monks were respected by Mohammedan and Christian alike. Patmos was left untouched in the Latin distribution of the islands in 1207, and remained nominally under Venetian suzerainty until the Turks gained control of the Aegean in the first half of the sixteenth century. Miller, speaking of the early fifteenth century, says, 'The one place in the Aegean which the Mussulmans never molested was the monastery of Patmos, whose monks were on the best of terms with them.'[39]

The monastery had always had the right to own ships, and had made the island a centre of trade for the eastern Mediterranean. Its period of greatest prosperity was from the time of the fall of the Duchy of the Archipelago in the 1540s until the middle of the seventeenth century. The Turks at this time allowed the monks to continue their trading activities and to use their ships to collect the rents and administer their estates in Crete and elsewhere. The monastery wielded considerable economic power and the island supported a community of wealthy shipowners, whose vessels travelled as far as Holland. The Turks, however, ravaged the island during the Venetian War of the 1660s, when it was used as a Venetian base. By the end of the seventeenth century Tournefort marvelled that the houses of so poor an island should be so well-built.[40] It recovered its prosperity to some extent in the eighteenth century, when the monastery provided a centre of Greek education, and its ships found new trade outlets with the Black Sea and Russia.

In Patmos the room was divided by a wooden partition, with the bed placed behind it. A bed tent therefore was not necessary, and the opening in the partition was filled with a curtain in the manner of the Cyclades. At the same time some curtains were provided with a gabled 'doorway' as in the Dodecanesian bed tent

[32]Tarsouli, *op. cit.*, pls. 56, 59, 25.
[33]Montesanto in *Dedalo*, vol. XI, 1930-31, p. 122.
[34]*Bibila* is the name given to a needle-made lace, usually consisting of small detached flowers worked in a chain, in bright naturalistic colours. When used as a dress edging, the flowerets were smaller and more formal. It was widely made round the coasts of Asia Minor and in the European provinces of the Turkish Empire generally.
[35]A. Hadjimichaeli, *Catalogue of an exhibition of Greek costumes and embroideries from the Benaki Museum, circulated by the Smithsonian Institution*, 1959-60, p. 33. For illustration of the costume see Tarsouli, *op. cit.*, pls. 15, 20.
[36]*Costumes et usages des peuples de la Grèce moderne*, 1825, pl. XXIV. The drawings were made in 1811.
[37]Savary, *Letters on Greece*, 1788, pp. 125-26.
[38]T. Oikonomidis, Ἡ γυναικέια φορεσιὰ τῆς Καρπάθου in *Laographia*, vol. 14, 1966, pls. II, III.
[39]W. Miller, *The Latins in the Levant*, 1908, p. 599.
[40]*A voyage into the Levant*, vol. I, p. 330.

[32, 33]. Another characteristic was that the embroidery was worked almost entirely in pattern darning. Dawkins has called this the Patmian stitch, but it was also widely used in the Cyclades and in Cos.

There is no doubt that very fine household embroideries were made in Patmos, but so many different types have at one time and another been attributed to the island that there is a good deal of confusion as to which of them were in fact made there. Wace states that there was a tradition in the island that the older embroideries were all in red,[41] and he favoured for this role King pattern curtains similar to those from Amorgos, but there is some doubt about this theory. Two red embroideries which may come from Patmos are illustrated at figs. 44, 45. It is also possible that the red Queen pattern curtains which Wace and Dawkins attributed to Milos may have been Patmian. The curtain 736-1877 [52] was said to come from that island when it was acquired by the Museum in 1877. Other embroideries which have been attributed to Patmos by some authorities have been assigned by others to Pholegandros, Naxos and Cos. In view of these conflicting theories one must ask whether the usual assumption of one island, one pattern is always valid, or whether, at any rate among certain islands, several patterns for bed curtains were current, to be worked at choice. The type of curtain which Wace and Dawkins attributed to Patmos and which is generally accepted as coming from that island is worked in a ground-covering arrangement of combined King and Queen patterns [33].

Astypalaia Astypalaia is the westernmost island of the Dodecanese and much of the varied embroidery shows a strong affinity with the Cyclades and a good deal of Italian influence. The island was not part of the domain of the Knights of St John, but became the fief of the Quirini family, under Venetian suzerainty, at the Latin division of the Aegean in 1207, and remained so until it fell to the Turks in 1540.

The costume of the island was extremely colourful. It consisted of a full-skirted under-dress with wide sleeves [34-37] worn under a sleeveless over-dress. Head-dress and 'stomacher' [38] were embroidered with metal thread and sequins and the long headscarf was also embroidered at the ends [39]. The sleeves were embroidered in vertical stripes, as in Nisyros and Tilos, and here also the patterns were given names, such as the 'centipede'. The sleeves also carried large 'blobs', worked in the threaded stitches of the Dodecanese, and called in this island *dixos* [34, 35]. (The two examples in the Museum collection have dixos patterns only and no embroidered stripes.) Similar patterns were worked on curtains. The borders at the wrists, however, were very finely embroidered in formal Renaissance patterns, left in reserve against a coloured background, which were decidedly Italian in character. Some of these sleeves, presumably the older examples, are made of very fine linen.

The skirts by contrast were made of heavy coarse cotton and the borders worked in bold cross stitch and bright colours [36, 37]. The patterns included all the Italianate motifs which were popular in the Cyclades – animals, birds, ships, female figures, etc. In Astypalaia the birds were known to the embroideresses as partridges and doves, and the animals as mules and camels. They are referred to in one of the island stories, which describes a girl embroidering a night-shirt for her husband. She puts on it: '. . . patterns of two sorts together, the pattern of horsemen and the centipede pattern. And this was not all: it was embroidered all over with fairies, with network, and with processions of riders and with camels and ships and doves and partridges and embroideries of all sorts.'[42]

Wace has suggested that this Cycladic style in an island of the Dodecanese was due to the importation of settlers from Tinos and Mykonos by Giovanni Quirini in 1413, after the island had been depopulated in a Turkish raid, but this action angered the Venetians and he was in fact obliged to return the uprooted populations to their own islands, which were at this time Venetian possessions.[43]

The skirts give a strong impression of the nineteenth century, but one of the border patterns (the partridge) is repeated in the Museum collection three times, one example in the normal large stitching and bright colouring, one on a smaller scale, and the third smaller still [36]. In this piece the cross stitch is fine and close and the colours sober. Is it to be regarded as earlier in date? And if so, are the apparently nineteenth century skirts coarse copies of an earlier fashion?

A headscarf [39] provides yet another contrast in that the pattern on the ends

[41]Wace, *Med. and N. E. embroideries*, p. 27.
[42]R. M. Dawkins, *Forty-five stories from the Dodecanese*, 1950, p. 29. The description is a composite catalogue of all the embroideries of the island. It could not apply to any actual man's shirt.
[43]Wace, in *Burlington Magazine*, vol. XXVI, 1914, p. 106. Miller, *The Latins in the Levant*, p. 600.
[44]Montesanto, *L'Isola dei Gigli*, pp. 40-1, figs. following p. 88. This book contains a full account of the costume of the island.

is taken from the famous Turkish mosque-and-cypress pattern, although in this case the building has a cross on top and is clearly intended to be a church or monastery. The pattern appears to have been a popular one, repeated on a number of these scarves, which are described by Marica Montesanto as christening scarves.[44] Another characteristic was the Byzantine eagle worked in the centre of the scarf.

A certain type of household embroidery from Astypalaia would also seem to have been produced in the nineteenth century. This included towels [40] and valances worked with the same Cycladic (or Italian) motifs as are found on the skirts, but here left in relief against a background of drawn thread work overcast in brightly coloured silk, a technique which is undoubtedly due to Italian influence and presumably indicates that these pieces stem from an older tradition. With the skirt borders, they seem to point to a nineteenth century revival of the craft in the island.

In complete contrast are a curtain [42] and valance worked in double running (holbein) stitch in red and blue with a stylized pattern of branching flowers. These were attributed by Wace to Astypalaia.

This is the only island from which samplers, which evidently acted as pattern books, survive. An example in the collection [41] includes a number of motifs from the skirt borders and shows the ground stitching of a dixos, on which the threaded stitches of the completed pattern would be worked.

THE CYCLADES

⁴⁵For illustrations see *Burlington
Magazine*, vol. XXVI, 1914, pp. 101-02,
and *Burlington Fine Arts Club Catalogue*,
1914, pl. 13.
⁴⁶Wace, *Burlington Fine Arts Club
Catalogue*, 1914, p. xvi.
⁴⁷See for example *Burato* by Alessandro
Paganino, published in the early
sixteenth century (ed. E. Ricci,
Bergamo, 1909).
⁴⁸*A voyage into the Levant*, vol. I,
pp. 218 ff.
⁴⁹J. L. S. Bartholdy, *Voyage en Grèce*,
vol. II, 1807, p. 99; Choiseul-Gouffier,
Voyage pittoresque dans l'empire Ottoman,
2nd ed., vol. I, 1842, p. 13.
⁵⁰Tournefort on Milos, *A voyage into the
Levant*, vol. I, p. 217.
⁵¹J. de Thévenot, *Relation d'un voyage
fait au Levant*, vol. I, 1664, p. 195,
description of Naxos.
⁵²*A voyage into the Levant*, vol. I, p. 219.
⁵³D. O. Dapper, *Description exacte des
Isles de l'Archipel*, 1703, p. 355;
Choiseul-Gouffier, *op. cit.*, p. 13.
⁵⁴See, for example, the curtains in the
Victoria and Albert Museum collection
T.267-1950 and T.261-1950; valance
T.347-1950; and cushion covers T.682-
1919 and T.694-1919.
⁵⁵Compare Hadjimichaeli, *L'art populaire
grec*, p. 101. This piece, T.641-1950, may
correspond to no. 422 in the Dawkins
manuscript catalogue, which was bought
in Astypalaia.

Our knowledge of the embroidery patterns of the Cyclades is less precise than in the case of the Dodecanese. Embroidery is attributed to only a very few of the many islands of the group, and at the same time a large number of pieces exist which are undoubtedly Cycladic but which cannot at present be given an island of origin.

The Cycladic bed alcove was at one end of the room. It was reached by steps, leaving a storage space beneath, and partitioned from the room by a wooden railing or by a curtain, or both.⁴⁵ The curtains consisted of three or four loom widths of linen, each embroidered with vertical borders, and often joined by ornamental openwork seams. Many curtains had a horizontal border of similar pattern at top or bottom. Wace believed those with the borders at the top to be the older. Valances were much shorter than in the Dodecanese, and were only one width deep. They were often used in pairs, and the derivation of a pair of valances from an ordinary bedspread has been explained as follows:⁴⁶ if a spread with embroidered borders was used on a bed platform with a wall at the back, one side of the spread obviously became superfluous, but if this side was folded over to the front of the bed, the embroidery was then inside out. The spread was therefore worked in two halves, which could be laid one over the other on the same side of the platform with the embroidery right side out on both pieces. Even so the embroidery at the ends of the two pieces was left overlapping, and to overcome this the ends of the top valance of a pair were folded inwards to reveal the valance below. This in turn meant that the ends of the top valance must be worked on the under side. (This arrangement is not as complicated as it sounds, see fig. 63.)

The embroideries of the Cyclades were invariably worked on the counted threads of the ground material in stitches which lend themselves to this technique, mainly darning, cross and satin. This meant that all the designs became stylized, even when they were based on natural objects such as birds and flowers. Except for the King pattern curtains of Amorgos, variations on the Queen pattern and conventional flower sprays were normally found on curtains. Confronted birds or stags, divided by a tree or flower vase, together with ships and eagles, were very usual on valances. The borders on cushion covers were often purely geometric in design [49-50, 66-69], and some of these patterns are also not unlike some of the formal designs printed in Italian sixteenth century pattern books.⁴⁷ Cycladic cushion covers are normally worked on only three, or even two, of the four sides, that is to say only the edges that showed when the cushions were piled on the bed were embroidered.

There is very little costume embroidery from the Cyclades in the Museum collection. The dress of many of the islands evidently resembled that of Mykonos, which was illustrated and described in detail by Tournefort.⁴⁸ Briefly, it consisted of an under-blouse with close fitting sleeves, a shift or under-dress with short full skirt and immensely long wide sleeves, turned back to the shoulder to show the under-blouse, a thickly pleated skirt, tied high under the bust and shorter again than the shift, a sleeveless bolero jacket, apron and headscarf, this last differently arranged in different islands. The essential features were the flowing sleeves, and the bulky, two-tiered, short-skirted silhouette, under which it was the fashion to thicken the legs to grotesque proportions with three or four pairs of coloured cotton stockings, supplemented with socks or gaiters to make the ankle and calf the same thickness.⁴⁹ The result met with the strong disapprobation of western travellers, who were universally agreed with Tournefort that the costume was 'very Disadvantageous to the Fair Sex.'⁵⁰ Thévenot, in the middle of the seventeenth century, tells us that 'ces femmes portent plus de dix robbes, l'une sur l'autre, de sorte qu'à peine peuvent elles cheminer.'⁵¹ Tournefort, however, says of Mykonos, 'Embroidery being an Invention of the Levant, they wear nothing without it: and to speak truth, they excel even the French in that sort of Work, as to Neatness; but their Patterns are not so well fancy'd.'⁵² His drawings of embroidery, however, are imprecise, and do not appear to correspond to any actual piece. Dapper also mentions an embroidered chemise in connection with Mykonos, and another traveller at the end of the eighteenth century speaks of red borders on the shifts of Kimolos, but in general references to embroidery are very rare.[53] Illustrations in Choiseul-Gouffier and Tournefort show that the under-dress of the Cyclades had a narrow embroidered border round the hem, which was continued vertically to a depth of four or five inches at each of the three seams, two in the front and one at the back [II]. One of these dress borders is illustrated at fig. 56.

Bed curtains in four or five traditional patterns, all worked in pattern darning or darning and satin stitch, have been variously assigned by different authorities to Patmos or to certain islands of the southern Cyclades, Amorgos, Milos, Phole-gandros. In the present state of our knowledge it does not seem possible to make more than tentative efforts to sort out this confusion.

Amorgos In the first place we have curtains and valances decorated entirely with vertical rows of King pattern leaves [43]. When these are worked in three colours, red, green and brown, it seems certain that they come from Amorgos. Curtains with the same pattern worked entirely in red were attributed by Wace to Patmos (p. 14) but we do not know what the all-red embroideries of Patmos were actually like, and it is possible that this particular type did in fact come from Amorgos. On the other hand pieces worked in the same pattern but in finer darning, and in reds and greens which correspond to colours used in Patmos, could well come from that island. The same doubts apply to cushion covers, which have the King pattern of Amorgos curtains but are often in one colour (green, black, etc.).[54] If the monochrome curtains come from Amorgos, presumably the cushion covers do also.

A characteristic of Amorgos curtains is a narrow edging border with a ball and triangle pattern, and this occurs on cushion covers of purely geometric pattern, of which two or three types may be attributed to the island [49, 50]. A number of cross stitch embroideries, all of the same pattern, were attributed by Dawkins to the district of Aigiali at the north-east end of the island [47]. Another type of valance [46], worked in a thick raised cross stitch reminiscent of Rhodian em-broidery, with a pattern of urns, plants and peacocks, is also tentatively attributed to Amorgos.[55]

II. Costume of the island of Ios, Cyclades. Reproduced from Choiseul-Gouffier, Voyage pittoresque dans l'Empire Ottoman, *2nd ed., 1842. The drawings were made in the 1770s.*

Amorgos was famous for a red dye made from a lichen which grows in many of the islands but was only used as a dye here. According to Tournefort this was known to Pausanias. In his own time the dye was still made and 'transported to Alexandria and England, where the Dyers use it.'[56]

Milos

Milos knew a period of prosperity in the seventeenth century, when the French corsairs used its fine natural harbour as a base and a clearing market for their booty, but their activities were proscribed by Louis XIV in 1673, and by the end of the eighteenth century Choiseul-Gouffier tells us that the old town, which was in an unhealthy situation, was nearly deserted, and the island was very poor.[57] A type of red curtain [52] with Queen pattern embroidery in darning was attributed by Wace and Dawkins to Milos, although Patmos has also been suggested (p. 14). A valance in the Dawkins collection which was made up from one of these curtains is known to have been acquired in Milos,[58] and it is possible that the attribution of these curtains to the island hangs on this one piece alone. A fragment in the collection has the same pattern in red and green, but this is unusual.

Another type of curtain which Hadjimichaeli attributed to Milos is also based on the Queen pattern, although the design is more complex. It is embroidered in darning and satin stitch in red, green and black. Wace gave this style tentatively to Pholegandros.[59]

An interesting valance [53] with a pattern of ships, which bears no resemblance to the curtains, was attributed to this island by Dawkins, who also mentions in his manuscript catalogue several polychrome pieces in satin stitch with a 'loose skinny pattern', which he attributes to Milos or Thira. It is not possible to identify these, but from the description they may be from Siphnos [58].

Pholegandros

It seems fairly certain that the Queen pattern border in satin stitch [54], which was presumably made for a curtain or valance, comes from Pholegandros. Another type of curtain, which is attributed by Greek authorities to Patmos, had a central band which is very similar, and side borders in a distinctive version of the King pattern. Such curtains were also tentatively assigned by Wace to Pholegandros, probably on the strength of the likeness to the satin stitch borders.[60]

Bent says that he saw exquisite gold and silver lace and lovely silk embroidery in the house of one of the old families of Pholegandros, but he does not describe the embroidery. He says the bed curtains were of 'striped silk gauze with gold lace insertion', and pillows of 'red silk, edged with gold lace'.[61]

Siphnos

Siphnos is another island where the embroideries were worked in satin stitch, on a fine linen with an open weave. Both the curtain [58] and the valance [57] are characteristic patterns.

Although Siphnos was ruled by a Spanish family, the da Corogna, through the fourteenth and first half of the fifteenth centuries, before passing to the Gozzadini of Santorin, the embroideries follow the normal Mediterranean/Italian tradition of the Cyclades and cannot be said to show any specifically Spanish influence.

Naxos

The island of Naxos became the capital of the Frankish duchy of the Archipelago in 1207 and did not finally fall under Turkish rule until 1580. In spite of this long association with Italian rulers, the very distinctive embroideries which are attributed to the island show no Italian influence. An embroidery known to have been acquired in Naxos which has the familiar Italian/Cycladic bird and animal decoration is probably of very late date.[62] It is, of course, possible, and even likely, that the red embroidery commonly associated with the island was not the only type of work done there, but, apart from this one piece, it is not possible to attribute any other type to Naxos with any certainty. The Dawkins manuscript catalogue attributes some drawn thread pieces, presumably white, to 'Ios, possibly Naxos'.

The famous red embroidery appears to have been made in enormous quantities [59-62]. More of it has probably survived than from any other island in the Aegean. Bent describes a visit to the village of Apeiranthos (in the mountains on the east side of the island), where he saw a great deal of red embroidery. He comments, 'Nowhere in Naxos is embroidery so common as here.'[63] From this it is clear that the village was an important centre for the embroideries, but it does not of course follow that they were not made elsewhere as well. It is found on

[56]*A voyage into the Levant*, vol. I, p. 182.
[57]*Voyage pittoresque . . .* , vol. I, p. 15.
[58]T.148-1950.
[59]Hadjimichaeli, *L'art populaire grec*, p. 105; Wace, *Med. and N. E. embroideries*, no. 22. The style is represented in the Victoria and Albert Museum collection by T.150-1950.

[60]Hadjimichaeli, *loc. cit.*; Wace, *Med. and N. E. embroideries*, nos. 21, 23.

[61]*The Cyclades*, reprint 1966, p. 204.

[62]The monochrome red embroideries were attributed to Naxos by Wace and Dawkins in the *Burlington Fine Arts Club Catalogue*, 1914, and have since been accepted by all authorities as worked in that island. A valance from the Wace collection (Liverpool City Museums 56.210.132) with a different type of Cycladic decoration was bought in the village of Apeiranthos. It compares to another piece in the same collection (56.510.133), which was made for a church and dated 1907 in the dedication, but not definitely known to have been acquired in Naxos.

[63]*The Cyclades*, reprint 1966, pp. 357-58.

[64]Wace, *Med. and N. E. embroideries*, p. 10.

[65]Compare for example Turkish silks such as Victoria and Albert Museum 744-1884, or Migeon, *La Collection Kelekian*, pl. 35.

[66]Wace, *Med. and N. E. embroideries*, p. 22; Hadjimichaeli, *L'art populaire grec*, p. 99.

[67]Wace, *Burlington Fine Arts Club Catalogue*, 1914, p. xv.

[68]T.715-1950, tentatively attributed to Anaphi, in coloured cross stitch. Dawkins catalogue, white valances attributed to Ios or Naxos, nos. 189-95.

curtains, valances and cushion covers, the latter being made in the form of a long runner with a narrow border all round. This was folded across the width and joined at the sides to form an oblong cushion cover. It is unlike embroidery from other islands in that the whole surface is covered with a repeating design. Because of this it lends itself to cutting to make smaller pieces, and large pieces are rare, while fragments are common.

Wace has described the traditional pattern as an adaptation of the double-leaf King pattern of Rhodes and Amorgos.[64] There is, however, an interesting unfinished fragment in the Dawkins collection [62] which has the design drawn on the back, and from this it is quite clear that the prototype was the classic Turkish silk pattern of a pomegranate between two leaves.[65] The repetition of the motif is so arranged that the leaves form a lattice with a pomegranate in the centre of each diamond. In the Naxiote adaptation the pomegranate has been repeated four times to each division of the trellis, thus falsifying the original conception of a fruit set in its own leaves. Apart from that, the technique of darning on the counted threads has resulted in a rigid stylization of the more naturalistic original, which has reduced all curves to straight lines, and produced a formal pattern which could hardly have been recognized without this fragment as a guide. The characteristic serrated lines of this type of silk design have been faithfully, if mechanically, reproduced, and have become in turn a feature of Naxiote embroidery. The fragment also shows that these embroideries were worked from the wrong side, which is not an uncommon technique in peasant embroidery.

The stylized leaf trellis is the basis of most Naxiote embroideries but many permutations on the pattern occur. One of the most usual is the omission of the trellis to leave a repeating pattern of isolated stars [60].

Wace was of the opinion that while the monochrome red embroideries were almost certainly from Naxos, embroideries of the same type with the addition of blue and green might come from some other island. Hadjimichaeli attributes a piece with this type of design but with the leaf trellis in a light colour to Patmos.[66] Rather similar embroideries with geometric designs, nearly always in two or three colours, worked much more coarsely and often used as border patterns only, come from the Northern Sporades [85].

Anaphi

From Anaphi we have a large number of valances with borders of the traditional animal decoration. A pattern based on the double-headed eagle [63] was particularly characteristic, and is found on towels from the island as well as valances. It is impossible to tell whether all similar valance patterns should in fact be attributed to Anaphi, or whether some may have come from neighbouring islands. The Dawkins manuscript catalogue, for example, suggests Pholegandros for certain unidentified valances which appear to be in the Anaphi style.

It is these valances which illustrate most clearly the method of turning in the ends of the top piece of a pair [63]. Most of them are in coarse cross stitch in bright colours, but one example in satin stitch from the Dawkins collection was acquired in the island [64]. Wace states that, according to information obtained in the island, the satin stitch embroideries were older than cross stitch, and as far as Anaphi is concerned this appears to be so.[67] It is also worth noting that this piece alone of the Anaphi valances in the collection is made entirely of linen, all the cross stitch pieces being worked on cotton or a linen/cotton mixture.

A number of cushion covers with geometric patterns are also attributed to Anaphi [66-69], and since each pattern illustrated is repeated on two or three examples, all appear to have been traditional. A characteristic of the cushion covers of this island is that they have an embroidered border along one end and up part of one side only.

Ios

Another border [70], which is attributed to Ios, has typical Cycladic decoration based on a pair of confronted peacocks with tails and bodies worked in satin stitch in a distinctive pattern. It is less weighty in design and technique than those from Anaphi. A cross stitch version of this pattern also exists, and it occurs again in white drawn thread work valances. It may be noted that the Dawkins catalogue attributes seven white valances, although not necessarily those with the peacock pattern, to 'Ios, possibly Naxos'.[68]

Mykonos

Only one piece in the collection is tentatively attributed to Mykonos [73]. It is probably part of a curtain, in white embroidery on fine white linen with motifs not unlike those of Siphnos. Angeliki Hadjimichaeli was strongly of the opinion that no embroidery was made in this island at all. This may have been true of household embroidery but, as we have seen from Tournefort's comment quoted on page 16, it cannot have applied to costume. Dawkins refers to several pieces in his manuscript catalogue which he attributes to Mykonos, in many cases because they were sold to him by a 'Mykonos man'. It has not been possible to identify these. Most of the embroideries mentioned appear to be polychrome, some of them with rose spray patterns and silver or gilt thread.

The costume of the island followed the short-skirted Cycladic type, but although Tournefort disapproved so strongly, it seems to have been very sumptuous. A visitor in the late eighteenth century explains this by saying that so many of the men had been carried off that the girls had difficulty in finding husbands, 'ed è forse per questa cagione che si studiano nell'arte delle attrattive, e s'abigliano e vestono con grandissimo lusso facendo uso ordinariamente di Velluti, e dorure' (and it is perhaps for this reason that they study the art of attraction, and they wear clothes of the greatest luxury, making use ordinarily of velvet and gold ornament).[69]

Kimolos

The embroideries tentatively attributed to Kimolos by Wace and Dawkins are curtains and valances with borders of rather primitive and angular rose spray patterns worked in loose surface darning within an outline of double running [74]. A similar curtain from the Myres Collection in the Ashmolean Museum is attributed to Kalymnos (p. 11, n. 31). The island appears to have been wretchedly poor, and Tournefort comments that the women 'have no other Employment but making Love and Cotton Stockings.' At the end of the century Choiseul-Gouffier also mentions the poverty of the village, and says the dress of the women is just a dirty mass of white linen: the petticoat is very short and embroidered in red.[70] No traveller, and many ships put in there, mentions embroidered curtains.

The Dawkins collection includes many of the coarse white-work valances with patterns of the Cycladic type which have already been mentioned [75, 76]. They are clearly copies of Italian models, but it is not certain that they all came from the Cyclades. In the same way borders with markedly Italian designs, worked in red or green cross stitch leaving the pattern in reserve, were evidently made in large numbers in the Cyclades and Ionian islands [77, 78]. Louisa Pesel states that those worked in green were said by the dealers to come from Ios,[71] but it could not be said with any certainty that they were made only there.

[69]Pasch di Krienen, *Breve descrizione dell'Arcipelago*, 1773, p. 83.
[70]Tournefort, *A voyage into the Levant*, vol. I, p. 112; Choiseul-Gouffier, *Voyage pittoresque . . .*, vol. I, p. 13.
[71]L. Pesel in *Burlington Magazine*, vol. X, 1907, p. 235.

[72]Hadjimichaeli, Ἑλληνικὴ Λαϊκὴ Τέχνη, Σκύρος, 1925, p. 130.
[73]*Voyage pittoresque . . .*, vol. I, p. 127. Choiseul-Gouffier visited the island in 1776. He remarks that there was nothing noteworthy in the houses or the costume except the custom of covering the walls with pots.
[74]Wace, *Med. and N. E. embroideries*, pp. 29-30.
[75]For illustrations of the gala dress and men's shirts, neither of which is represented in the collection, see Hadjimichaeli, Ἑλληνικὴ Λαϊκὴ Τέχνη, Σκύρος, pls. 58, 60, 136, and for further examples of border patterns, pl. 116. See also Benaki Museum, *Skyros embroideries*, 1965, pls. 22-6.
[76]Hadjimichaeli, *op. cit.*, p. 141. *Burlington Fine Arts Club Catalogue*, 1914, no. 128.
[77]Wace, *Med. and N. E. embroideries*, p. 31. Hadjimichaeli, in *Byzantinisch-Neugriechische Jahrbücher*, vol. 12, 1936, pp. 116 ff.

THE NORTHERN ISLANDS

The Northern Sporades   The embroideries of the Northern Sporades are usually attributed to Skyros, but it is impossible to say if in fact they were made only there or if the same type was also made in Skopelos and Skiathos. It is worth noting that these last two islands are said to have been completely depopulated after the capitulation to the Turks at the end of the 1530s, and in other cases where this happened there is often no tradition of embroidery in the island concerned.

Characteristic Skyros embroideries are heavily influenced by the floral style of Turkish faience from Isnik and Chanakkale,[72] and also include large numbers of birds, ships and human figures, particularly men in Turkish dress, which during the eighteenth century also became the normal male dress of the Aegean islands. The Northern Sporades changed hands between Franks and Byzantines in the period following the Fourth Crusade, but came into Venetian possession after the fall of the Byzantine Empire in 1453 and remained so until the capitulation of Skyros to the Turks in 1538. There seems therefore to be no particular historical reason to explain the choice of Turkish rather than Italian models here, but certainly during the eighteenth century there was a tradition of decorating the houses with pottery from the mainland. Choiseul-Gouffier mentions the custom of hanging pots on the walls, but says nothing about the embroideries.[73]

The embroideries are on bedspreads (not valances) made of three widths of linen, with isolated motifs round the borders [79-81]. It is thought that those with large motifs were older than those with smaller versions.[74] There are numerous small square cushions [83], and long cushions in two main styles, the first with a bold floral pattern [82] and the second with horizontal rows of small motifs or figures. In the women's costume the hem of the under-dress is embroidered with small motifs very like the patterns on the bedspreads. The bodice of the gala costume was in dark red or blue silk with elaborate gold embroidery in the Turkish style on the cuffs of the wide sleeves. The only traces of Italian influence in these islands are in white drawn-work patterns on the sleeves of the shepherds' shirts and in the very narrow borders in holbein stitch which finished the edges of the under-dresses.[75]

In addition to the freely drawn patterns, a number of cushions with geometric border patterns very much in the style of Naxos were found in the Northern Sporades [85]. They are, however, usually much coarser than the Naxos examples, and worked in two or three colours, while the method of making up the cushion also differed from the Naxos type. (The cover consisted of a single loom width of material with identical embroidered bands at each side and in the centre. This was folded through the centre band and joined at the outer edges, so that each face of the cushion showed one outer band and half the centre one.) Angeliki Hadjimichaeli considered that at least some of those found in Skyros were brought there from outside, and it seems likely that the pattern was copied there and became a subsidiary style in the island. A piece exhibited in the Burlington Fine Arts Club Exhibition of 1914 combines the traditional Skyros style with a 'Naxos type' pattern.[76] Other cushion patterns are tentatively attributed to the Northern Sporades owing to the similar arrangement of the borders [86-87].

Wace has suggested that so many embroideries of the freely drawn Skyros type [81] were found in the northernmost islands of the Cyclades that embroidery in this style must have been made there. He chooses Paros as the most likely centre, on the grounds that the dialect of Paros is of the northern Aegean type, and that similar dialects and embroidery styles often go together. Hadjimichaeli disagreed with this theory, and in fact no confirmation of it has since come to light, so for the time being all these embroideries are attributed to Skyros.[77]

Thasos   Long cushion covers embroidered with ground-covering geometric patterns [88] were attributed by Wace to Thasos, but these are the only embroideries thought to come from this island.

Chios   Chios was a prosperous island, which not only produced silk but supported a flourishing silk weaving industry from the fourteenth to the early nineteenth century which exported figured silks to the mainland. It may be that with silk materials readily available, the inhabitants felt no need to create elaborate embroideries, but whatever the reason there is little embroidery from Chios, most of it on minor articles of dress. The women's costume included a square scarf or kerchief pinned over the very low décolletée, and examples of two traditional patterns are included in the collection [89-90]. The costumes and embroideries of Chios, and the history of the silk industry there, have been exhaustively discussed by Philip Argenti.[78]

Mytilini   Certain white embroideries [91], which are worked mainly in satin stitch, in silk with a little silver thread, are attributed to Mytilini by Hadjimichaeli, but it would be rash to suggest that this type of embroidery came only from this island. Wace also suggested for Mytilini a type of coloured border consisting of small flowerets [93]. This pattern was often found on scarves, but one piece in the collection may have been a curtain.

Samos   The island of Samos was completely evacuated by the inhabitants owing to Turkish pressure after the fall of Constantinople in 1453. It remained uninhabited for some eighty years and was then repopulated by the Turks with immigrants from other parts of Greece and the islands, but even at the beginning of the seventeenth century it was described as 'quasi deshabitée et déserte pour craincte des Corsaires.'[79] The present-day inhabitants maintain that the various sections of the immigrant population brought with them the embroidery styles that they knew, and that it is for this reason that no particular style can be attributed to the island. It does in fact appear that there was no embroidery tradition in Samos.

[78]*The costumes of Chios*, 1953.
[79]H. de Beauvau, *Relation journalière d'un voyage du Levant*, 1608, p. 106.
[80]Wace, *Med. and N. E. embroideries*, p. 19. A piece in the collection acquired from Professor Newberry (1185-1903), which he had obtained in Cairo, is described, presumably by him, as a Kalamata towel.

Certain towels or scarves [94, 95] which are traditionally attributed to Argyrokastro (Gjinokaster), now in southern Albania, have elements in their patterns which are rather like the coloured borders mentioned above, which may come from Mytilini. Wace stated that examples of these towels had been found in Chios and Rhodes, and it therefore seems at least possible that they came from one of the islands near the coast of Asia Minor. Kalamata has also been suggested as a place of origin.[80]

EPIRUS AND THE IONIAN ISLANDS

In western Greece, that is to say in the mainland district of Epirus and in the Ionian islands off the coast, we find embroideries which differ in technique, being worked on the one hand in darning and on the other in cross stitch, but which are in some cases very close indeed in design. (Compare, for example, the darned bedspread [96] with the cross stitch spread [105].) Most cross stitch examples came without any doubt from the Ionian islands, but authorities have differed regarding the origins of the darned embroideries.

Historically the two regions were divided by the course of the Turkish conquest, which engulfed the northern areas of mainland Greece during the late fourteenth and early fifteenth centuries. Epirus then remained Turkish until its return to the Kingdom of Greece in 1912, with the exception of the towns of Butrinto, Parga, Preveza, Vonitza and Arta, which were the dependencies of the different rulers of the Ionian Islands. They changed hands between Venetians and Turks on various occasions from the late fifteenth to the late eighteenth centuries. The capital, Joannina, which fell to the Turks in 1430, became the seat of a pashalik, and with the advent of the famous Ali Pasha in 1788, enjoyed considerable prosperity as a focal point for trade and communications and as a centre for the luxury crafts.

The Ionian Islands, with one exception, remained virtually throughout in western hands. After a varied history under Byzantine, Sicilian, Angevin and Neapolitan rulers, all the islands eventually passed to Venice. Corfu became Venetian in 1386, and Cephalonia, Zante and Ithaka some hundred years later, after a few brief years under the Turks. Only Levkas (Santa Mavra) remained Turkish from 1479 until it returned to Venice late in the seventeenth century.

Two classes of embroidery are attributed by all authorities to the Ionian Islands: cross stitch borders, mostly on bedspreads and dresses [105, 106], and drawn thread work interspersed with darned motifs [108-110], which is usually on cushion covers but is also used for borders. In the first, motifs of the Italian/Mediterranean type, such as confronted peacocks divided by a fountain or a tree, recur constantly, as they do in Cycladic borders. The drawn thread work also is obviously directly influenced by Italy. It is not, however, possible to attribute definitely any of the various types within these classes to any one island or village, with the exception of certain cross stitch cushions [113, 114], which are thought to come from Corfu. Wace states that the drawn thread work was largely found in Cephalonia and Zante, and that cross stitch bedspreads were found in Cephalonia and Corfu, and it is clear from a statement in the Dawkins manuscript catalogue that the dealer from whom he had some of his Ionian embroideries had acquired them in Cephalonia.[81] On the other hand the Benaki Museum in Athens attributes both these types to Levkas.

Some linen under-dresses in the Ionian islands had embroidered wrists and hems which correspond to the borders on the household embroideries, but again ·it is not possible at present to attribute them to any particular island. The French consul Grasset de St Sauveur, who served in the Ionian islands late in the eighteenth century, describes the costumes but is not specific about the embroidery. He tells us that the countrywomen of Corfu adopted 'les ornemens de la dorure et de la broderie,' but the costume of Levkas appears to have impressed him most. Of this he says, 'Les femmes . . . sont singulièrement portées pour la parure et le luxe. Leur costume, ainsi que celui des hommes, est à l'oriental: elles ne négligent rien pour le rendre riche. Tous leurs habits sont ornés de broderies à la Turque, en or, en argent, et en soie. Leurs chemises, les culottes longues et larges qu'elles portent sous leurs jupons, sont également brodées. La chemise nuptiale est de soie blanche, brodée au bas et autour de la gorge, en or et en argent: c'est un présent du marié.'[82] Some fine under-dresses or shifts in the Benaki Museum, which have elaborate white embroidery the whole length of the sleeve, are attributed to Levkas.[83]

In Corfu it would seem that the bed was decorated with lace rather than with coloured embroidery. A writer in the middle of the nineteenth century says, 'One circumstance, however, attracts the attention of strangers, and that is the size and beauty of their beds. This peculiarity arises from their not being seizable for debt . . . In former days, the working of bed-linen occupied the young women's

[81]Wace, *Med. and N. E. embroideries*, pp. 16-7. The cross stitch bedspread borders in the Victoria and Albert Museum, T.230 to 237-1950, can all be identified with Dawkins manuscript catalogue numbers, and all are said to have been acquired in Cephalonia.
[82]Grasset de St Sauveur, *Voyage historique, littéraire et pittoresque dans les isles et possessions ci-devant vénitiennes du Levant*, 1799-1800, vol. II, pp. 197, 353.
[83]There is no dress of this type in the Victoria and Albert Museum collection. For illustration see Benaki Museum, *Epirus and Ionian Islands embroideries*, 1965, pl. 24.

time till their marriage; and, consequently, it was profusely ornamented with a coarse description of lace, very much resembling old point lace. A far more delicate sort was worked, chiefly for presents to churches, but the custom is now nearly extinct.'[84]

The disputed darned embroideries are very like those of Asia Minor, with the difference that the latter are composed almost entirely of regular repeating floral patterns, which were certainly inspired by a desire to emulate woven silks, while the Greek examples are more varied. They include pots of branching flowers and birds and animals, as well as human figures. They are worked on household items such as bedspreads (or divan covers) with embroidered borders, cushion covers and some towels. Sir Henry Holland, who visited Joannina in 1812-3, describes the houses: 'Bed chambers are not to be sought for in Greek or Turkish habitations. The sofas of their living rooms are the place of nightly repose with the upper classes: the floor with those of inferior rank. Upon the sofas are spread their cotton or woollen mattrasses, cotton sheets and ornamented quilts.'[85] Another traditional use for embroidery seems to have been as a hanging over the chimney breast.[86] The finest pieces among these embroideries are long cushion covers with wedding scenes, of which there is no example in this collection.[87]

Wace originally thought that these embroideries should be attributed to Joannina, taking into account the Turkish influence in the designs and the mixed population of Epirus, but later reconsidered this opinion in favour of the Ionian islands, evidently feeling that the similarities between them and the Ionian cross stitch pieces were so great that they must have a common place of origin. He puts forward the theory that the darned embroideries were the older form in the Ionian islands, which gave way to the easier cross stitch, as evidently happened in Anaphi.[88] Angeliki Hadjimichaeli, on the other hand, maintained very strongly that the darned embroideries came from Epirus. She accounts for the likenesses between the two types by the close communications between the two areas, relationships between families, intermarriage, and so on.[89]

The most telling points in Mrs Hadjimichaeli's argument are the markedly Turkish style of the darned embroideries, which, given the respective history of the two areas, would certainly seem to point to an Epirote origin, and the evidence of the marriage cushions. These tally exactly with her description of Epirote marriage customs, and this is borne out by an account in Hobhouse. He makes it clear that the celebrations took much the same form elsewhere in Greece, but says that they found the ritual more elaborate (and in his eyes more ridiculous) in Joannina.[90] Mrs Hadjimichaeli also claims that the men's costume shown in the marriage cushions,[91] which was undoubtedly of Turkish origin, was formerly the costume of the Epirote bourgeois.

If the costume of the cushions was in fact Epirote costume of the sixteenth century, it does not of course follow that all the embroideries, or even the cushion covers themselves, should necessarily be dated as early as this, since the pattern, once established, could have continued as a tradition well after the fashion in actual dress had changed.

Although it may be accepted that some at least of the darned embroideries, and particularly the marriage cushions, are from Epirus, certain questions remain to be answered. Technically three distinct groups may be distinguished, all of which have very similar motifs: firstly, the marriage cushions, and darning which is very similar in technique and colouring [96, 98]. Secondly, darning which leaves a longer stitch on the surface, and is worked in a soft floss silk of satiny appearance in particularly bright colours [97]. It is possible that this should be regarded as a later version of the first group. Thirdly, darning worked on the counted threads to produce regular diagonal lines [99, 100]. A distinctive feature of this type is the diamond shapes left in reserve on the bodies of animals, etc. Individual motifs in all these embroideries are very close to those found in the cross stitch and drawn thread work of the Ionian islands.

In the present state of our knowledge it is impossible to say whether all these embroideries were made all over Epirus, or whether certain types should be assigned to certain districts, or whether in fact some could have been made in the Ionian islands. The particularly close relations of the coastal towns with the islands might perhaps account for similarities in the patterns. It is possible that the distinction between cross stitch in the islands and darning on the mainland is

[84]H. J. W. Jervis, *History of the Island of Corfu*, 1852, p. 266.
[85]H. Holland, *Travels in the Ionian Islands, Albania, Thessaly and Macedonia*, 2nd ed., 1819, p. 228.
[86]A. Hadjimichaeli in *Byzantinisch-Neugriechische Jahrbücher*, vol. 12, 1936, pp. 112-13. She cites Wace, *Med. and N. E. embroideries*, no. 14 (pls. XX, XXI) as an example. This piece is some 3 × 2 ft, embroidered all over with a haphazard arrangement of birds, flowers, etc. See also fig. III for illustration of such a hanging.
[87]For illustration see Wace, *Med. and N. E. embroideries*, nos. 12, 13 (pls. I, II, XIX).
[88]Wace, *Burlington Fine Arts Club Catalogue*, 1914, p. xiii; *Med. and N. E. embroideries*, pp. 16-9.
[89]Hadjimichaeli in *Byzantinisch-Neugriechische Jahrbücher*, vol. 12, 1936, pp. 97-118.
[90]Lord Broughton (J. C. Hobhouse), *Travels in Albania*, 2nd ed., vol. I, 1858, pp. 152-53.
[91]It consists of tight trousers with boots and a short tunic, covered by a long surcoat frogged at the front, with short wide sleeves showing the narrow sleeves of the tunic. Compare Turkish military costume as illustrated for example by Vecellio, *Degli abiti antichi e moderni*, 1590, pp. 397-98.
[92]Hadjimichaeli (*op. cit.*, p. 114) states that some cross stitch embroideries were made in the neighbourhood of Joannina which were almost identical with the Ionian ones.

too sharply drawn.[92] There also seems to be no reason to think that either cross stitch or darning was of earlier date than the other in this particular region.

A different type of embroidery which is attributed by all authorities to Joannina consists of divan covers and cushion covers with floral patterns worked in herringbone stitch [101, 102]. These patterns, especially those based on the rose spray design, also show strong Turkish influence. Spreads of this type appear to have been made by joining separate embroidered borders to a plain centre, and in almost all extant examples the borders have been removed from the centre and joined to each other to make a coverlet embroidered all over.

Yet another category closely linked to the herringbone embroideries consists of divan covers made in this way and embroidered either in a mixture of herringbone and darning or in some cases entirely in darning. All these pieces appear to be made to one particular pattern, which is closely related to a Turkish pomegranate silk design. The example in the Museum collection is entirely in darning, while the colouring and the simplification of the design suggest that it may be of later date than those worked in both stitches [104].

A very finely worked under-dress or shift, showing Turkish influence in the silver flower spray at each side of the neck opening, is also attributed to Epirus [103].

THE GREEK MAINLAND

With the exception of Epirus, embroideries from the Greek mainland are almost entirely on dress. Under-dresses were embroidered in coloured silks, as in the islands, and jackets for men and women were elaborately embroidered in gold. These last were made in professional workshops, and also by travelling tailors who went from village to village.[93]

The gold embroidered garments in the collection include four of the handsome women's sleeveless coats which were worn by the bourgeois classes in Joannina, as well as in other towns of northern Greece, Albania, Montenegro and Hercegovina. Two of these (895-1902 and T.3-1920) belong to costumes from Scutari (Shkoder) in Albania, and none could be directly attributed to Joannina, although this town was a famous centre for professional gold embroidery in the late eighteenth and nineteenth centuries, and exported garments as far afield as Bosnia and Montenegro. Other gold embroideries are a man's jacket and waistcoat from Albania (652 to c-1904), two jackets from Corfu (453 and 454-1877), and a jacket of the type introduced by Queen Amalia of Greece and worn as national court dress in the mid-nineteenth century (424-1889). A man's short jacket and waistcoat, embroidered not in gold but with couched cords, is of the type worn with the fustanella, the white kilt of the Albanian and Epirote mountains. This costume spread into Attica and the Peloponnese: the jacket and waistcoat are said to come from Patras but could be attributed to the Peloponnese in general rather than any one town in particular (455 and a-1877).

III. Costume and interior, Joannina.
Reproduced from T. S. Hughes,
Travels in Greece and Albania, *1820.*

Unfortunately mainland costume is not adequately represented in the Museum collection. Coloured embroidery on costume was worn in many districts, including the large off-shore island of Euboea, and also by the nomadic Sarakhatsan tribes who inhabited the northern parts of the country.

A fine complete costume from Attica is illustrated at fig. 117. It is thought to come from Keratea, south-east of Athens, but the same costume was evidently worn all over Attica. As late as 1907 it was accurately described by the American P. S. Marsden, who visited the village of Menidi on a feast day: 'Their robes were in the main of white, but the skirts were decked with the richest of woollen embroideries, heavy and thick, extending for several inches upward from the lower hem, in a profusion of rich reds, blues and browns. Aprons similarly adorned were worn above. Most impressive of all, however, were the sleeveless overgarments or coats . . . of white stuff, bordered with a deep red facing and overlaid with intricate tracery in gold lace and gold braid.'[94]

The embroidery on an under-dress from Corinth is in rather similar style, which is very different from the island patterns (T.207-1922). An interesting sleeve from Doliana in Arcadia (Peloponnese) has a pattern very similar to the King pattern of the Dodecanese, and the colours, red, brown and blue, also correspond, although they are darker in tone [118]. It is thought that immigrants from the Dodecanese may have been responsible for the similarity.[95] Minor items of mainland costume include dress borders from Arachova near Delphi and the neighbourhood of Marathon, while three unusual cushion covers are composed of a patchwork of scraps of dress embroidery from Macedonia (T.718-1919, T.719-1919, T.234-1912).

Embroidered dresses from the village of Trikeri are again in the island style [119, 120]. Trikeri lies at the extreme tip of the Mount Pelion peninsula. The inhabitants emigrated to the present site when they were driven from the islet off the peninsula now known as Old Trikeri (Palaio Trikeri) by pirate raids. According to the traveller L. Bartholdy this evacuation took place only a few years before his visit there in 1803-4. He describes the settlement on the peninsula as a wealthy village with a port which was one of the busiest on the east coast of Greece.[96]

The embroidery on the under-dresses consists of stylized flower sprays or birds and is very close to the patterns on Skyros dresses. (The Northern Sporades lie just outside the mouth of the Gulf of Volos and are geographically very near the Trikeri peninsula.) In Trikeri the hems of the dresses were finished with a narrow beading of multicoloured satin stitch, while in Skyros they had narrow edging borders of small geometric patterns. As in Skyros, festival dresses were made of red or blue silk, and the colour changed with a woman's status as she became betrothed, bride, married woman and widow.[97]

[93]Zora, *Embroideries and jewellery of Greek national costumes*, p. 13.
[94]*Greece and the Aegean Islands*, 1907, p. 142.
[95]The sleeve compares to dresses in the Benaki Museum, to whom I am grateful for this explanation.
[96]J. L. S. Bartholdy, *Voyage en Grèce*, 1807, pp. 172 ff. Henry Holland (*Travels in the Ionian Islands . . .*, 1812-13, vol. II, pp. 93-4) also speaks of Trikeri as 'very modern'.
[97]Hadjimichaeli, Κεντήματα τοῦ Τρίκερι, 1951, p. 14.

CRETE

The Cretan embroideries acquired by Thomas Sandwith while he was Consul-General in Crete probably constitute the earliest collection of embroideries from the Greek islands to be preserved.

While most of the surviving embroideries from other islands are on household articles, much of the best work in Crete was on costume, especially on skirt borders. These skirts were embroidered in silk in brilliant colours and a large number of stitches, of which the most widely used was Cretan feather [121-124]. Other borders, frequently narrower than the polychrome examples, were worked entirely in dark red or dark blue [125-127].

Although the designs differ greatly in detail, their main components are constant and fall into two well-defined categories, one based on a frieze of flower vases [121], and the other on a trellis of detached diagonal leaves [123]. Both these motifs were widely used in Italian silks of the seventeenth century which, since Crete remained in Venetian hands until 1669, could well have provided the inspiration behind the embroideries.[98] These basic patterns are thickly interspersed with additional flowers and foliage and a large number of beasts, birds and insects, and in some cases human figures. A siren rising from the flower vase is very characteristic, and can also be traced to Italian influence.

The skirts were very full, being made normally of five loom widths of a linen and cotton material, and were suspended from the shoulders by short straps, so that the gathers fell from above the bust [127]. 'They tye their petticoats and aprons near as high as their armpits', says one traveller in the middle of the eighteenth century.[99] Cretan skirts are the only embroideries which were sometimes signed and dated by the worker (p. 9).

Apart from these well-known floral skirts three quite different types of pattern are represented in the Sandwith collection. Although the possibility that these were pieces brought from other islands must be taken into account, the facts that

IV. Costume of Crete. Reproduced from J. Pitton de Tournefort, A voyage into the Levant, 1718.

they were worked on the traditional linen/cotton mixture, and that in two cases they were made up into skirt borders in the characteristic manner argue strongly that they were made in Crete.[100]

The first is a group in red cross stitch, sometimes outlined in green [128]. The patterns are based on a hexagon, and bear a strong resemblance to designs in Italian pattern books of the sixteenth century.[101] Secondly, there is a border with a brightly coloured repeating pattern based on a stylized flower form, worked in double darning outlined in black [129]. The third pattern is also worked in red, in pattern darning, and consists of a band of diaper pattern, surmounted by a row of peacocks [130].[102]

A complete dress in the Sandwith collection, which is a very rare example of its kind, is also cut so that a full gathered skirt falls from above the bust, in this case from a low round neckline [131]. Immensely long gathered sleeves also fall from the neck. The only embroidery, which shows a bride and her attendants in a border of flowers, is on the sleeves. The dress, which may have come from the neighbourhood of Canea,[103] probably dates to the nineteenth century, but the style was evidently very much older. A description by an Irish monk on pilgrimage to the Holy Land in 1322 must refer to such a dress. He says: 'Judeorum vero et grecorum mulieres ibidem ornatum habent valde singularem, quia quedam suppelliciis velut latinorum clerici chorales induuntur. . . .' (In the same city [Candia] the Jewish and Greek women wear a very peculiar dress, since some of them are clad in surplices like those of Latin choir clerks).[104]

It has never been satisfactorily established how the skirts were worn. The description which accords best with them is Tournefort's, but even he, acute observer as he was, does not mention embroidery. He says, '[The women] . . . are but queer Pieces; their Habit discovers no Shape, which yet is the best thing about them. This Habit is very plain: a sort of an upper Coat of reddish Cloth, full of Pleats, hung on the shoulders by a couple of Thred-Laces; their bosom is left quite bare.'[105] If this description is taken in conjunction with his drawing [IV] it would appear that the 'upper coat' was worn over an under-dress with wide sleeves. It is possible that the embroidered skirts were a bridal or festival version of this plain dress, since the description tallies apart from the colour and the decoration.

The skirt borders in the Sandwith collection are thought to have come from the district of Sphakia in the south-west of the island,[106] and there is evidence to show that the costume of this district in the late eighteenth and nineteenth centuries was basically of the same cut although it was of much lighter material.[107] Another skirt, which is cut in the characteristic style but made of fine material, in this case pure linen, could well have been part of this costume. The narrow band of embroidery at the hem, worked in pastel coloured silks and metal threads, is entirely Turkish in style and technique [133], and this accords with the comments of the German traveller Sieber early in the nineteenth century, who said that in his day the dress illustrated by Tournefort was only worn by old women and a few girls in the towns, while most of the women had adopted Turkish fashions.[108] The Turkish fashions also included long full trousers. A pair which is not from the Sandwith collection but compares to a pair of trousers acquired by him and now in possession of the Sandwith family is shown at fig. 134.

In this later costume the bare shoulders of earlier centuries were covered by the koleto [136, 137]. This fichu or tippet of fine linen or silk gauze is well represented in the Sandwith collection. All the examples are decorated with insertions of Cretan bobbin lace, and some are embroidered in silk and metal thread, either with floral patterns or with satin stitch embroidery which appears to derive from Italian sixteenth century models. The name colletto also suggests that the garment goes back to the Venetian period, that is prior to 1669, although Tournefort and his contemporary the Dutch traveller Dapper both mention the low décolletage at the turn of the century.

There is less emphasis on household embroidery in Crete. A few large hangings or bedspreads exist, embroidered in the style of the polychrome skirts. Cushion covers in two varieties are much commoner. On both there is floral embroidery which is again in the style of the skirt borders. Small rectangular cushions have in general a central motif which can include human figures, surrounded by a border with diagonal flower sprays in the corners [137]. A frequent feature of long cushion covers is a border of 'lappet' patterns at each end [138]. 'Lappets' also occur on

[98]See for example Victoria and Albert Museum 952-1887, 1031-1900, or Flemming, Encyclopaedia of Textiles, 1958, pls. VI, 109, 87.

[99]Pococke, A description of the East, 1743-45, vol. II, p. 266.

[100]For a fuller discussion of these pieces see P. Johnstone in Apollo July 1972, pp. 62-8.

[101]For example, Domenico da Sera, Opera nova . . . , Venice, 1543.

[102]The examples of this pattern in the collection (т.636 & 637-1950, fig. 130) are not Sandwith pieces, but compare to a Sandwith skirt border now in the possession of his family.

[103]A pair of sleeves in the Benaki Museum which compare to this dress were acquired in Halepa near Canea in 1906.

[104]Symon Simeonis, quoted by D. Hemmerdinger-Iliadou in Studi Veneziani, vol. IX, p. 550.

[105]A voyage into the Levant, vol. I, p. 67.

[106]Sandwith himself left no information with the collection, but his daughter, in correspondence with the Museum in 1931, made it clear that she believed the embroideries to have come from this district.

[107]The sketch shown at fig. V tallies with a description of Sphakiote costume given by G. Papadopetrakis, Ἱστορία τῶν Σφακίων, 1877, p. 55.

[108]F. W. Sieber, Reise nach der Insel Kreta, vol. II, 1823, p. 327.

[109]Wace, *Med. and N. E. embroideries*, p. 33; Victoria and Albert Museum, *Brief guide to Turkish woven fabrics*, 1950, pl. 20.

skirt borders, and they have been likened by Wace to Italian lace patterns of the seventeenth century. Very similar end borders were woven on Turkish velvet cushions of the same period.[109]

Several cloths or cushion covers in the Sandwith collection have borders embroidered with flower patterns in the Turkish manner. One illustrated at fig. 139 has in the centre a woman, probably a bride, standing in a church door. Both the costume of this figure and the embroidery technique compare to a cushion in the Benaki Museum which is decorated with a border of girls dancing.

V. Sketch in pastels entitled 'Candia' from a collection of original costume drawings by Georg Graf von Rumpf, some of which are dated 1768-69. Reproduced by courtesy of the Gennadius Library of the American School of Classical Studies at Athens.

CYPRUS

Two types of Cyprus embroidery are represented in the collection by two fine bedspreads, both of which were acquired in the village of Levkara. Both styles clearly derive from Italian sixteenth century models, the first in red cross stitch from the traditional wave pattern border [140], which also occurs frequently in Italian household embroidery, and the second in white work from *punto tagliato* [141]. The zigzag pattern in this border is very typical of the Cypriot style, which is much less elaborate than the Italian originals. Levkara whitework was revived in this century as a cottage industry to provide articles for sale.

Some rectangular cloths in the collection which were acquired in Cyprus are made of fine cotton with embroidered borders obviously copied from the traditional Turkish rose spray pattern. Headscarves and towels with embroidery of this type were very common everywhere in the Aegean and for the most part are not included in this survey because of the difficulty of distinguishing between Greek and Turkish work. These particular examples are less finely embroidered than genuine Turkish pieces and do not share their characteristic of showing both faces of the embroidery alike. They are described by M. H. Ohnefalsch-Richter as veils or shawls.[110] Travellers in the eighteenth and nineteenth centuries comment on the Turkish fashions worn by the ladies of Cyprus. G. Mariti, in the 1760s, says: 'The people clothe themselves in the same manner as the inhabitants of Constantinople. The ladies are distinguished by nothing but their light and lofty headdress. . . . [This] is an assemblage of beautiful printed muslin handkerchiefs, arranged so as to form something like a helmet; to the extremities of which they affix another handkerchief folded into the shape of a triangle, and suffered to float over the shoulders. This kind of helmet raises them a foot and a half. . . .'[111] Another traveller early in the nineteenth century also comments on the Turkish fashions worn by the ladies of Larnaca.[112] The embroidered cloths, from their technique, may be dated to the nineteenth rather than the eighteenth century.

[110]M. H. Ohnefalsch-Richter, *Griechische Sitten u. Gebräuche auf Cypern*, 1913, pls. 59, 72.
[111]G. Mariti, *Viaggi per l'Isola de Cipro*, 1769, trs. Cobham, *Travels in the Island of Cyprus*, vol. I, 1909, p. 10.
[112]C. C. Frankland, *Travels to and from Constantinople in the years 1827 and 1828*, vol. I, 1829, p. 318.

BIBLIOGRAPHY

Argenti, P. *The costumes of Chios*. London, 1953.

Bellinger, L. Κρητικὰ κεντήματα τῆς Συλλογῆς τοῦ Μουσέιου Ὑφαντῶν τῆς Washington in *Kritika Chronika*, vol. IV, Herakleion, 1950, pp. 264-67.

Benaki Museum. *Hellenic national costumes*. Athens, 1948-54.

—. *Epirus and Ionian Islands embroideries*. Athens, 1965.

—. *Skyros embroideries*. Athens, 1965.

—. *Crete, Dodecanese and Cyclades embroideries*. Athens, 1966.

Burlington Fine Arts Club. *Catalogue of a Collection of old embroideries of the Greek Islands and Turkey*. London, 1914.

City of Liverpool Museums. *Catalogue of an Exhibition of Mediterranean embroideries lent by Professor Wace*. Liverpool, 1956.

Gentles, M. *Turkish and Greek Island embroideries from the Burton Yost Berry Collection in the Art Institute of Chicago*. Chicago, 1964.

Gerola, G. 'I costumi muliebri nelle tredici Sporadi' in *Emporium*, vol. XXXVII, Bergamo, 1913.

Hadjimichaeli, A. Ἑλληνικὴ Λαϊκὴ Τέχνη Σκύρος. Athens, 1925.

—. Μεσογειακὰ καὶ Ἐγγὺς Ἀνατολῆς Κεντήματα in *Byzantinisch-Neugriechische Jahrbücher*, vol. XII, Berlin, 1936, pp. 97-118.

—. *L'art populaire grec*. Athens, 1937.

—. Κεντήματα τοῦ Τρίκερι. Athens, 1951.

—. (ed. Tatiana Ioannou). *The Greek Folk Costume*. English edition, Athens, 1979.

Johnstone, P. *Greek Island embroidery*. London, 1961.

Montesanto, M. 'Il ricamo nelle Sporadi Meridionali' in *Dedalo*, vol. XI, Milan, 1930-31, pp. 102 ff.

—. *L'Isola dei Gigli (Stampalia)*. Rome, 1932.

National Bank of Greece. *Greek Handicraft*. Athens, 1969.

Ohnefalsch-Richter, M. H. *Griechische Sitten u. Gebräuche auf Cypern*. Berlin, 1913.

Oikonomidis, T. Ἡ γυναικεία φορεσιὰ τῆς Καρπάθου in *Laographia*, vol. XXIV, Athens, 1966.

Papantoniou, I. Ἑλληνικες Φορεσιες (Greek Costumes) 2 volumes, Athens 1973-4. Summary in English and French.

Peiridhou, A., articles on Cyprus embroidery (in Greek) in *Kypriakai Spoudai*, Nicosia, vol. 14, 1950, pp. 163-84, vol. 17, 1953, pp. 57-66, vol. 20, 1956, pp. 67-72, vol. 22, 1958, pp. 253-59, vol. 23, 1959, pp. 187-209.

—. *Cyprus Embroidery*. Nicosia, 1976. (English translation from the above articles).

Tarsouli, A. *Costumes grecs*. Athens, 1941.

—. *Embroideries and costumes of the Dodecanese*. Athens, 1951.

Wace, A. J. B. *Mediterranean and Near Eastern embroideries from the Collection of Mrs. F. H. Cook*. London, 1935.

—, and Dawkins, R. M. 'Greek embroideries I & II' in *Burlington Magazine*, vol XXVI, London, 1914, pp. 49, 99.

Zora, P. *Embroidery and jewellery of Greek national costumes*. Athens, 1966.

Measurements given in the captions are for the whole object, not the details photographed

1. Part of a bed tent. Dodecanese, Rhodes. Silk on linen, cross stitch. Side panels red and blue. Door panel red, two shades green, blue, yellow, buff and cream. Length 263 cm. Width at bottom, door panel 90 cm., side panels each 40 cm. Misc.10-1921

2. *Detail fig. 1.*

3. *Detail from a bed tent door. Dodecanese, Rhodes. Silk on linen, cross stitch. Red, blue, two shades green, two shades yellow, tan, two shades fawn, cream. Dawkins manuscript catalogue no. 428 and Burlington Fine Arts Club Catalogue, 1914, no. 29, attributed to Rhodes in both cases. 276 × 51 cm.*
Dawkins Collection. T.660-1950

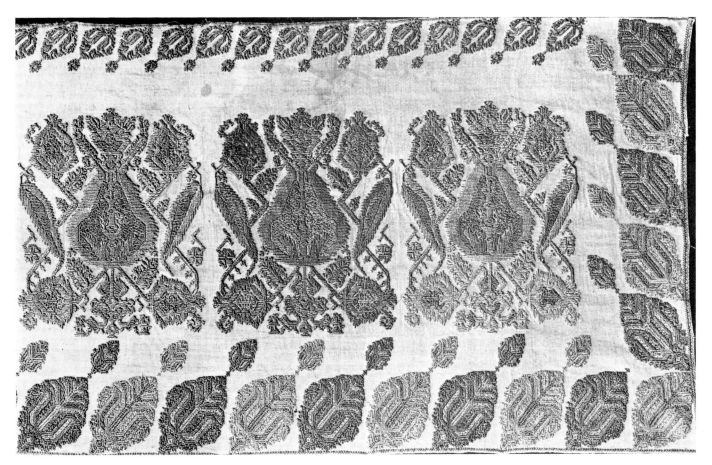

4. Detail from a bed valance. Dodecanese, Rhodes. Silk on linen, cross stitch. Red and green. 278 × 68.5 cm. T.287-1920

5. Detail from a bed valance. Dodecanese, Rhodes. Silk on linen, cross and double running stitches. Red and green. The bottom row of diagonal leaves is a later addition in the embroidery style of the Cyclades. 221 × 150 cm.   Dawkins Collection. T.464-1950

6. *Detail from a bed valance. Dodecanese, ? Rhodes. Silk on cotton, cross, long-armed cross, split and buttonhole stitches. Red and green, later additions in purple, turquoise, plum red and green. Tassels in purple and green at lower corners and centre lower edge. Nineteenth century. 158 × 53 cm. Dawkins Collection. T.665-1950*

7. Cushion cover. Dodecanese, Rhodes.
Silk on linen, cross and long-armed
cross stitches. Edges finished with a
couched cord, the two faces joined with
Cretan feather stitch. Red, blue, green,
yellow and buff. The underface is
embroidered with a similar border but
has no central cross. 44 × 39 cm.
Dawkins Collection. T.557-1950

8. Cushion cover. Dodecanese, Rhodes.
Silk on linen, cross, long-armed cross
and feather stitches. Embroidered on
both faces. The two faces joined by an
insertion stitch. Red, green and blue.
Purple and green tassels on two corners
are later additions. 51 × 46 cm.
Wace Collection. T.681-1919

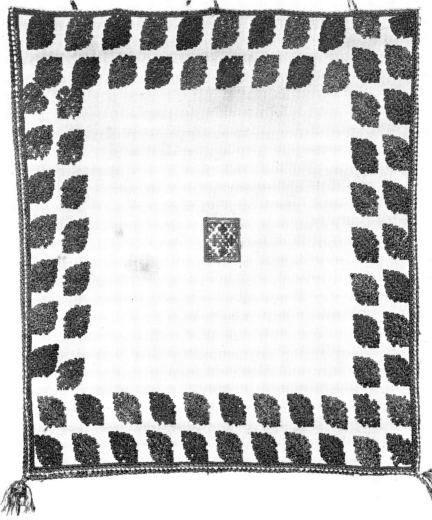

9. *Under-dress. Dodecanese, Rhodes. Silk on linen with groups of cotton warps, cross, split, buttonhole and threaded stitches and hem-stitching. Bodice and sleeve seams joined with faggoting, skirt seams with Cretan feather stitch to a depth of 25 cm. Hem, sleeves and neck finished with a plaited cord. Red, green, two shades yellow, black and pink. Nineteenth century. Length 104 cm. Width across sleeves 138 cm. Dawkins Collection. T.679-1950*

10. *Bed tent. Dodecanese, Cos. Eleven tapering panels with separate door panel added. Side panels embroidered in silk on linen, darning stitch. Red and green. The panels joined with strips of cotton woven in red and white stripes. Door panel, silk and metal thread on linen, darning, satin, cross, chain, double-running, tent and eyelet stitches. Red, green, blue, grey, shades of yellow and buff. At one time in possession of the Platanistas family of Cos. Length 331 cm. Width of side panels at bottom 39 cm. Length of door panel 251 cm. Width 51 cm. 67 & 68-1902*

11. Detail from fig. 10.

12. Detail from fig. 10.

13. Panel from a bed tent.
Dodecanese, ? Cos. Silk on linen,
cross stitch. Red and green.
236 × 31 cm.   Dawkins Collection.
T.374-1950

14. *Detail from a bed valance.*
Dodecanese, ? Cos. Silk on linen,
Italian two-sided cross stitch. Red
and green. 91 × 49 cm.
Dawkins Collection. T.661-1950

15. *Detail from a bed valance.*
Dodecanese, ? Cos. Silk on linen,
cross stitch. Red (faded to brown)
and green. Dawkins manuscript
catalogue no. 412, acquired in
Smyrna and attributed to Cos.
Nisyros or Symi are possible
alternatives. 226 × 45.5 cm.
Dawkins Collection. T.375-1950

41

16. *Border from a cushion cover. Dodecanese, ? Cos. Silk on linen, cross and long-armed cross stitches. Red, green, blue and yellow. 43 × 9.5 cm.* T.3-1909

17. *Detail from a cushion cover. Dodecanese, ? Cos. Silk on linen, cross and long-armed cross stitches. Red, blue, green, yellow, buff and cream. Embroidery the same on both faces. 49.5 × 40 cm.* *Dawkins Collection.* T.550-1950

18. *Detail from a cushion cover. Dodecanese, ? Cos. Silk on linen, cross and long-armed cross stitches. Red, green, yellow, buff and black. Embroidery the same on both faces. This piece was illustrated in the Burlington Fine Arts Club Catalogue, 1914, (no. 26) and there attributed to Cos with a query. 49 × 44 cm.* *Dawkins Collection.* T.127-1950

19. Detail from a bed valance. Dodecanese, Nisyros. Wool and silk on cotton, cross, chain and stem stitches. Coloured tassels on three sides. Red, blue, two shades green, two shades yellow, pink, mauve, tan, two shades buff. 171 × 43 cm.
Dawkins Collection. T.732-1950

20. Border from a cushion cover. Dodecanese, Nisyros. Silk on cotton, cross stitch. The two faces joined by an insertion stitch and buttonholing. Blue, yellow, buff, green, brown and black. 43 × 41.5 cm. T.166-1931

21. Border from a cushion cover. Dodecanese, Nisyros. Silk on cotton, cross stitch. The two faces joined by an insertion stitch. Brown, blue, yellow and buff. The colouring was described by Wace as typical of cushion covers and some valances from this island. 44 × 43 cm.
Dawkins Collection. T.577-1950

43

22. *Under-dress. Dodecanese, Tilos. Silk and silver thread on linen and cotton (skirt cotton, sleeves linen with cotton warp stripe). Cross, long-armed cross, chain, darning, satin and threaded stitches. Cretan feather stitch on the sleeve seams and the skirt seams to a depth of 20 cm. Gathers at the waist of the skirt are held by smocking. Neck and hem finished with a plaited cord, sleeves with four small tassels. Length 112 cm. Width across sleeves 138 cm. Dawkins Collection.* T.677-1950

23. Detail from a bed valance. Dodecanese, ? Tilos or Rhodes. Silk on linen, cross and long-armed cross stitches. Red and green. 165 × 85 cm. Dawkins Collection. T.115-1950

24. Detail from a bed valance. Dodecanese, ? Karpathos. Silk on silk. Cross and long-armed cross stitches. Red and green. This is a three width valance, the two lower widths joined by an insertion of gold braid. The ground material corresponds to the Karpathos dresses, figs. 25, 26. 218 × 104 cm. Dawkins Collection. T.662-1950

25. *Dress. Dodecanese, Karpathos. Silk on silk, cross, long-armed cross and stem stitches. The seams decorated with a form of Cretan feather stitch. Red, blue and green, with small amounts of yellow, black and white in the seams. Neck, sleeves and hem are finished with a plaited braid. The dress is made in one piece, but a very deep tuck has been taken in the skirt so that it has the appearance of a separate skirt and tunic. This dress was acquired by Theodore Bent in 1884 in Karpathos, where he was told that it had not been worn for a hundred and fifty years. According to his information this was the 'best' dress and the pattern was called* spertonato *(a hybrid Greek/Italian word presumably meaning 'the seed pattern'). Length 147 cm. Width across sleeves 159 cm.   346-1886*

26. *Dress. Dodecanese, Karpathos. Silk on silk, threaded stitches with long-armed cross, satin, chevron, tent and stem stitches. The seams decorated with a form of Cretan feather stitch. Red, blue, green and black, with small amounts of yellow and white in the seams. The cut is the same as 346-1886 (fig. 25) and the dress was acquired by Theodore Bent at the same time. The pattern was called* staphylato, *'the grape pattern', and was the 'second best'. Length 129 cm. Width across sleeves 136 cm.   348-1886*

47

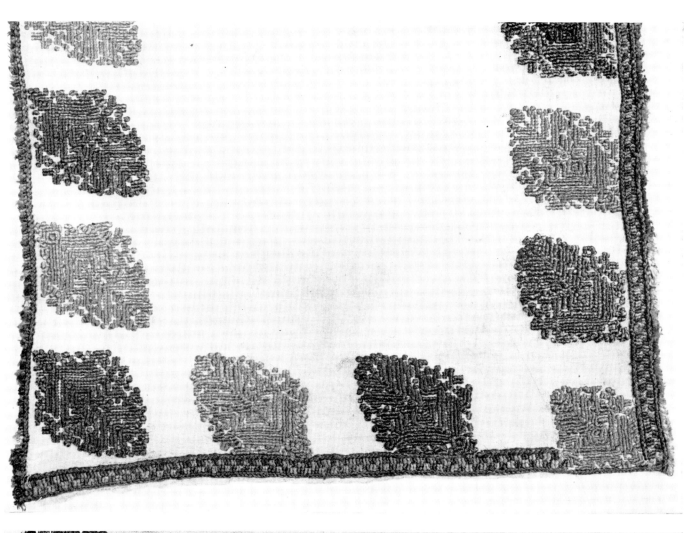

48

29. Under-dress. Dodecanese, Kalymnos. Silk on linen woven with groups of cotton warp stripes, cross, long-armed cross, double running, satin and Cretan feather stitches. The neck opening trimmed with openwork and bibila lace. Red, green, pale blue, yellow, salmon pink, shades of buff, outlining in black. Acquired in Kalymnos by W. R. Paton. Length 138 cm. Width across sleeves 151 cm.   331-1887

27. Cushion cover. Dodecanese, Karpathos. Silk on silk, cross, long-armed cross and stem stitches. The back of the cushion cover, now missing, was originally joined to this face with an insertion stitch. Red and green. 43 × 40 cm.   Dawkins Collection. T.560-1950

28. Sleeve of an under-dress made up as a cushion cover. Dodecanese, Karpathos, or neighbouring island. Silk on cotton. Threaded stitches with Roumanian, chevron, chain and stem stitches. The seam is decorated with a form of Cretan feather stitch and the join at the lower edge finished with a plaited braid and tassels. Red, blue, green, black, yellow and white. The use of cotton as a ground material suggests that the dress was not as old as 346- and 348-1886 (figs. 25 & 26). 46.5 × 39.5 cm.   Dickens Collection. T.143-1966

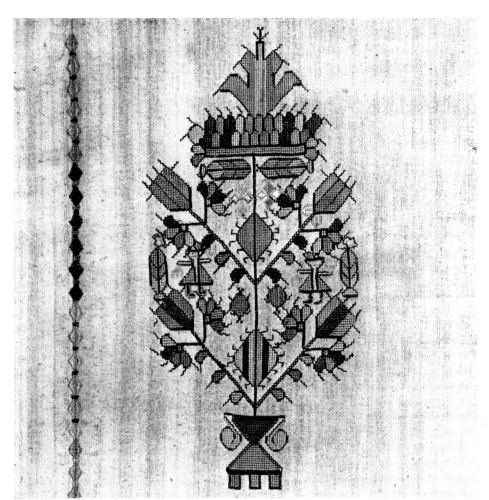

30. Detail from embroidery from an under-dress. Dodecanese, Kalymnos. Silk on linen, cross, double running, satin and feather stitches. Pastel colours with black outlines. Acquired in Kalymnos by W. R. Paton. 573-1886

31. Detail from a bed valance. Dodecanese, Kalymnos. Silk on cotton, cross stitch and double running. Red, two shades blue, yellow, shades of buff. 247 × 67 cm. Dawkins Collection. T.370-1950

32. Part of the door panel of a bed curtain. Dodecanese, Patmos. Silk on linen, darning, satin, cross and long-armed cross stitches. Red, green, cream and white. The style of the gable of this door panel, as well as the filling patterns on the birds and the inclusion of small dog-like animals, seems to compare to curtains of the type of T.654-1950 (fig. 33) usually attributed to Patmos, rather than to the Coan type gable illustrated by the Platanistas door panel (fig. 10). 143 × 38 cm.   A. Maudslay Bequest. T.92-1931

33. Part of a bed curtain. Dodecanese, Patmos. Silk on linen, darning, satin and chain stitches. The seam joined with an insertion stitch. Red, green, two shades of buff, some white. 279 × 81 cm. Dawkins Collection. T.654-1950

34. *Bodice of an under-dress. Dodecanese, Astypalaia. Silk and silver thread on linen, cross, two-sided Italian cross, Cretan feather and buttonhole stitches. The seams decorated with insertion stitches. Red, green, light blue, slate blue, yellow and pink. Length of bodice 43 cm. Width across sleeves 181 cm. Dawkins Collection. T.106-1950*

35. *Part of a sleeve from an under-dress. Dodecanese, Astypalaia. Silk on linen, two-sided Italian cross, Cretan feather, stem and running stitches. The seam joined with an insertion stitch. Part of the lower edge finished with a twisted cord. Sleeve patterns red, border light blue and yellow. 48.5 × 61 cm. Circ.317-1929*

36. *Detail from a skirt border. Dodecanese, Astypalaia. Silk on cotton, cross, buttonhole and back stitches. The seam joined with an insertion stitch. Red, blue, green, two shades yellow, slate and black. The pattern, which according to Marica Montesanto is called locally 'partridges left and right', is on a smaller scale than is usual in these skirt borders. Length 88 cm. Width round hem 168 cm.   Dawkins Collection. T.103-1950*

37. *Detail from a skirt border. Dodecanese, Astypalaia. Silk on cotton, cross, buttonhole and back stitches. The seam joined with an insertion stitch. Red, blue, green, black, yellow, mauve, and pink. Nineteenth century. Acquired in Astypalaia. Length 86.5 cm. Width round hem 183 cm.   Dawkins Collection. T.101-1950*

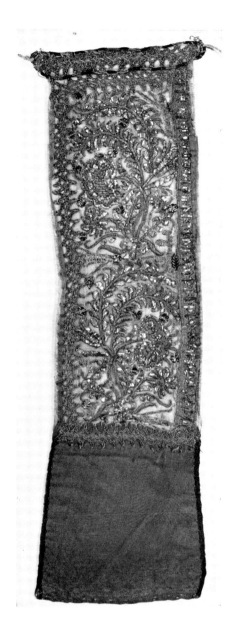

38. Stomacher. Dodecanese, Astypalaia.
Silver and silver-gilt threads and
sequins on cotton gauze. End tab of red
satin. Originally in the Bent collection.
38 × 10 cm. T.150-1930

39. Detail from a scarf. Dodecanese, Astypalaia. Silk and silver thread on silk. Cross, two-sided
Italian cross, woven hem-stitching and buttonhole stitches. Blue, green, black, yellow, orange and
pink. The 'monastery' design is a derivation of the Turkish 'mosque and cypress' pattern. The
double-headed eagle in the centre is characteristic of these scarves, which Marica Montesanto
refers to as christening scarves. 188 × 44 cm. T.2-1923

40. *Detail from a towel. Dodecanese, Astypalaia. Silk on silk, drawn thread work, cross and buttonhole stitches. Green, pink, blue and yellow. Nineteenth century. 174 × 43 cm. Dawkins Collection. T.222-1950*

41. *Sampler. Dodecanese, Astypalaia. Silk on cotton, cross, running and double running stitches. Red, blue and buff. The patterns worked in running stitches are unfinished, the running being a groundwork for the threaded stitches which would complete them. All the motifs are found on the dresses of the island. 46 × 43 cm.* T.221-1927

42. *Detail from a curtain. Dodecanese, Astypalaia. Silk on linen, double running and buttonhole stitches.* Red, blue and green. *206 × 119 cm.* Wace Collection. T.685-1919

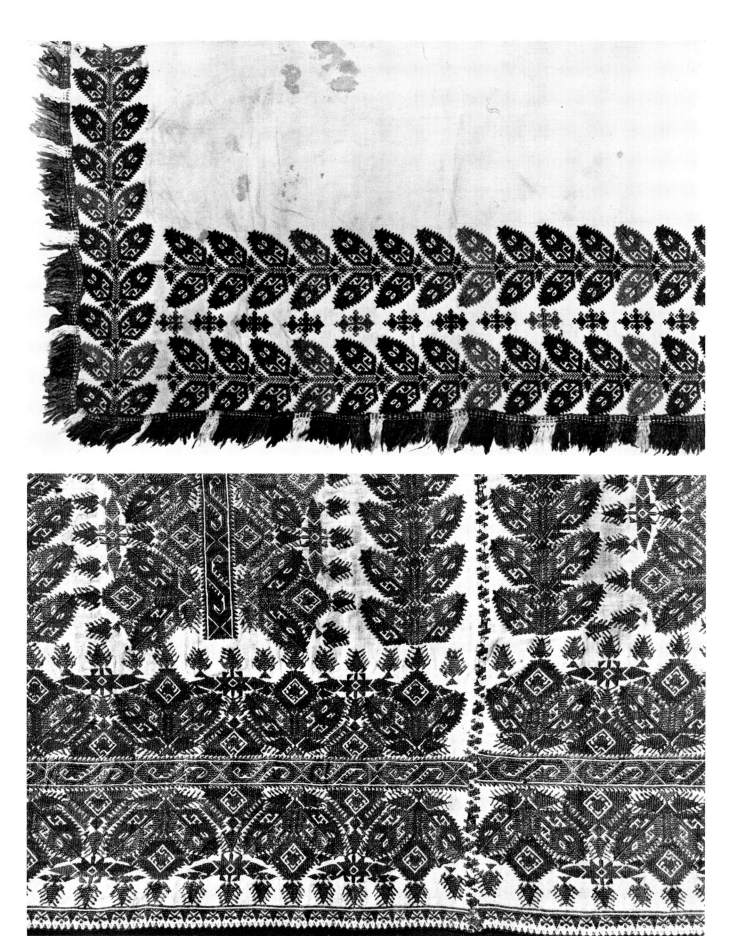

43. *Detail from a bed valance. Cyclades, Amorgos. Silk on linen, darning and cross stitches. Red, green and black. Coloured silk fringe. This piece is typical of the alternate colouring 'King' pattern bed furnishings of Amorgos.* 184 × 45 cm. *Dawkins Collection.* T.723-1950

44. *Fragment of a bed curtain. ? Cyclades, Amorgos. Silk on linen, darning stitch. Red, the seam joined with an insertion stitch in red and white. This curtain and fig. 45 could have come from Patmos (p. 14).* 51 × 74 cm. *Wace Collection.* T.690-1919

59

45. *Fragment of a bed curtain. ? Cyclades, Amorgos. Silk on linen, darning stitch. Two shades red. This curtain and fig. 44 could have come from Patmos (p. 14). 68 × 47 cm. Dawkins Collection.* T.268-1950

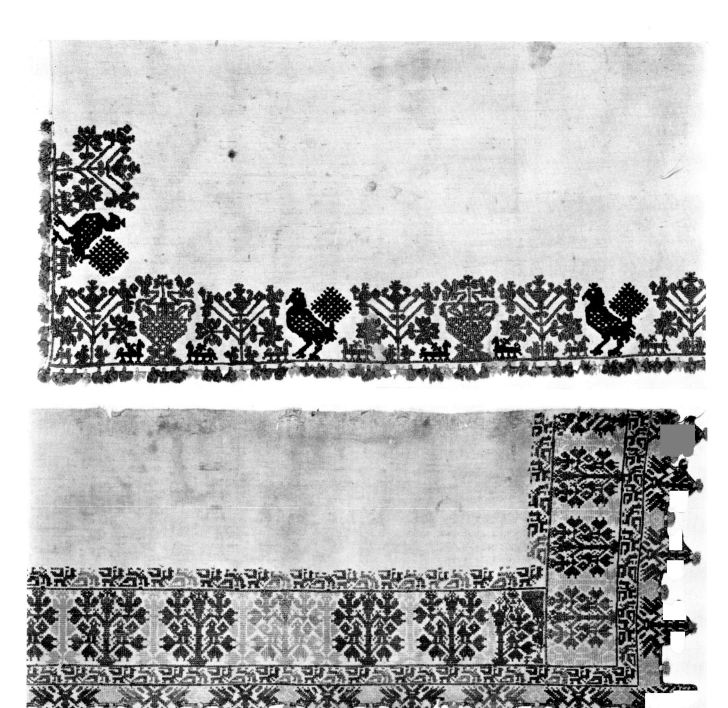

46. *Detail from a bed valance. ? Cyclades, Amorgos. Silk on linen, cross stitch. Red, green and black. Fringe of coloured silk tassels. A similar piece was attributed to Amorgos by Hadjimichaeli, but it is possible that this valance should be identified with no. 422 in the Dawkins manuscript catalogue, of which he says, 'Astypalaia, bought there'. 241 × 56.5 cm. Dawkins Collection. T.641-1950*

47. *Detail from a bed valance. Cyclades, Amorgos. Silk on cotton, cross stitch. The edge finished with buttonhole stitch and silk tassels. Red, blue and yellow. The pattern compares to a curtain attributed by Dawkins to the district of Aigiali at the north-east end of the island. 218 × 45 cm. Dawkins Collection. T.649-1950*

48. *Cushion cover. Cyclades, Amorgos.*
Silk on linen, darning stitch. Red, blue,
yellow. Both faces embroidered alike.
Cushion covers of this type correspond
to the 'King' pattern curtains
attributed to Amorgos. 58.5 × 42.5 cm.
Wace Collection. T.682-1919

49. *Cushion cover. Cyclades, Amorgos.*
Silk on cotton, darning stitch. Red, blue,
black and green. Both faces embroidered
alike. 36 × 43 cm.
Dawkins Collection. T.216-1950

50. *Cushion cover. Cyclades, Amorgos.*
Silk on linen and cotton, darning stitch.
Red, green, slate blue. Both faces
embroidered alike. The serrated border
pattern is found on curtains and cushion
covers from Amorgos such as T.682-1919
(fig. 48). 27 × 39.5 cm.
Dawkins Collection. T.218-1950

51. Detail from a curtain. Cyclades, island unknown. Silk on linen, satin and darning stitches. Monochrome red. 174 × 236 cm. T.140-1930

52. *Detail from a bed curtain. ? Patmos or Milos. Silk on linen, darning and satin stitches. Monochrome rose red. The seams joined by an insertion stitch in red and white. This curtain was described as 'from the Isle of Patmos' when it was acquired by the Museum in 1877, but see pp. 14, 18. 306 × 147 cm.   736-1877*

53. *Detail from a bed valance. Cyclades, Milos. Silk on linen, cross, stem and double running stitches. Rose red, two shades of blue, green, tan, shades of yellow and buff, black. Finished with a coloured silk fringe. The original design apparently consisted of ships and horsemen: other motifs were later additions. Attributed to Milos in the Dawkins manuscript catalogue, no. 118. 183 × 62 cm.   Dawkins Collection. T.346-1950*

54. *Detail from a border. Cyclades, Pholegandros. Silk on linen satin, darning, cross, long-armed cross and chain stitches. Red, blue, slate blue, green, yellow and brown. 35 × 19 cm. Given by Miss May Morris.* T.121-1939

55. *Detail from a border. Cyclades, Milos. Silk and metal thread on linen, satin, chain and double-running stitches. Monochrome red. The edges finished with tassels of pink silk and metal thread. Attributed to Milos in the Dawkins manuscript catalogue, no. 819. 56 × 11 cm. Dawkins Collection.* T.447D-1950

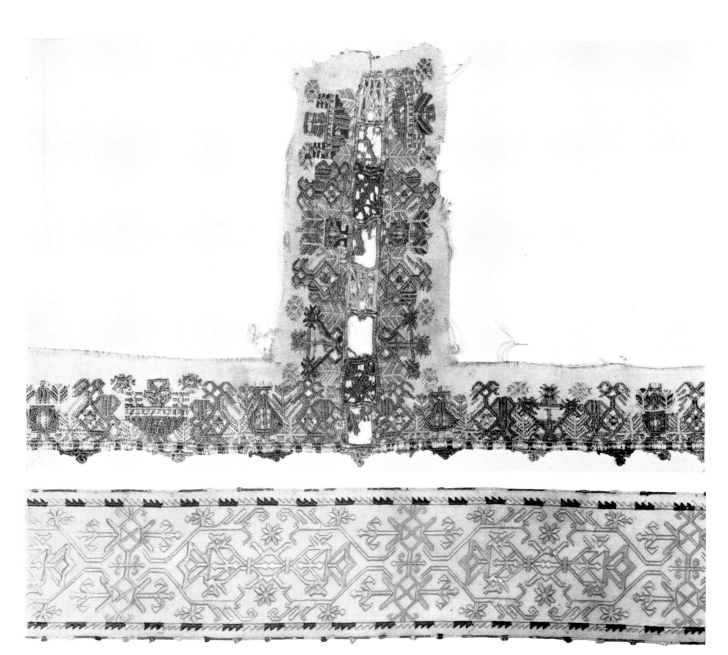

56. *Detail from a dress border. ? Cyclades. Silk on cotton, satin, double running and buttonhole stitches. The seams joined with a buttonhole insertion stitch, the edge trimmed with needlemade* bibila *lace. Red, blue, green, pink, yellow. The ornamented seams on this border are characteristic of under-dresses from the Cyclades, but the island is not known. Total length 166 cm. Dawkins Collection. T.672-1950*

57. *Detail from a border. Cyclades, ? Siphnos. Silk on linen, satin stitch. The edges finished with tassels, now largely worn away. Yellow, blue, some brown, and cream. Attributed to Siphnos with a query in the Dawkins manuscript catalogue, nos. 577-8. 262 × 10.5 cm. Dawkins Collection. T.442-1950*

58. *Part of a bed curtain. Cyclades, Siphnos. Silk on linen, satin stitch. Red, blue, green, two shades yellow. A curtain of this type is attributed to Siphnos by Hadjimichaeli (L'art populaire grec, p.101). 162 × 172 cm. Wace Collection. T.693-1919*

59. *Detail from a cushion cover. Cyclades, Naxos. Silk on linen, darning stitch. Red and blue. 127 × 49.5 cm. Dawkins Collection. T.179-1950*

60. *Part of a curtain. Cyclades, Naxos. Silk on linen, darning stitch. Monochrome red.*
94 × 43 cm. Given by Miss Baxter. T.230-1912

61. *Detail from a cushion cover. Cyclades, Naxos. Silk on cotton, darning stitch. Two shades*
of red. 111 × 39 cm. Dawkins Collection. T.178-1950

62. *Fragments of a cushion cover. Cyclades, Naxos. Photographed from the back, showing the drawing of the design on the back of the material. The embroidery is unfinished, and must have been worked from the wrong side. Silk on linen, darning stitch. Monochrome red. The lower border in cross stitch has been added and appears to be from another island. 49 × 41 cm. Wace Collection. T.676-1919*

63. *Pair of bed valances. Cyclades, Anaphi.*
Silk on cotton, cross and long-armed cross
stitches. Red, two shades blue, two shades
green, two shades yellow, pink, fawn and
black. Polychrome silk fringes. The valances
are arranged to show the layout of the em-
broidery as it appeared in use (p. 16). These
valances correspond to the Dawkins
manuscript catalogue nos. 117 and 124 and
were there attributed to Pholegandros. Upper
valance 171 × 49 cm. Lower valance 183 ×
50 cm. Dawkins Collection. T.605 and
608-1950

64. *Detail from a bed valance. Cyclades,*
Anaphi. Silk on linen, satin stitch. Red, two
shades blue, green, fawn, yellow. Silk fringe
in blue and fawn. The use of satin stitch
and the linen ground material may indicate
an earlier date than most surviving valances
from this island. One of a pair bought in
Anaphi in 1907. 184 × 49.5 cm.
Dawkins Collection. T.130-1950

65. *Detail from a bed valance. Cyclades,*
? Anaphi. Silk on cotton and linen (cotton
warp, linen weft), cross and long-armed cross
stitches. Red, blue, green, yellow, shades
of fawn. Polychrome silk fringe. 183 × 55.5
cm. Dawkins Collection. T.718-1950

66. *Border of a cushion cover. Cyclades, Anaphi. Silk on cotton, cross and long-armed cross stitches. Red, blue, green, two shades yellow, black. Corresponds to a piece from the Wace collection (T.691-1919) which is attributed to Anaphi – probably by Wace himself. 57 × 33 cm. Dawkins Collection. T.121-1950*

67. *Border of a cushion cover. Cyclades, Anaphi. Silk on cotton, cross and long-armed cross stitches. Blue, green, yellow, two shades pink, black. Both faces embroidered alike. Probably Dawkins manuscript catalogue no. 526, of which he says 'Anaphi certain'. 51.5 × 34 cm. Dawkins Collection. T.142-1950*

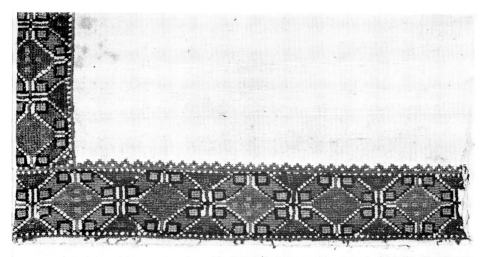

68. *Border of a cushion cover. Cyclades, Anaphi. Silk on cotton, cross and long-armed cross stitches. Red, blue, green, yellow, black. Both faces embroidered alike. This piece corresponds to cushion covers from the Wace collection bought in Anaphi, and also to nos. 75, 76 & 181 from the Wace collection illustrated in the Burlington Fine Arts Club Catalogue, 1914, attributed to Anaphi. It could also be one of Dawkins manuscript catalogue nos. 564-67 of which he said 'Pholegandros ? Anaphi ?' 47 × 35 cm. Dawkins Collection. T.582-1950*

69. *Border of a cushion cover. Cyclades, Anaphi. Silk on cotton, satin, cross and long-armed cross stitches. Red, blue, green, yellow. The bottom edge trimmed with three silk tassels. This piece is probably a pair to a cushion cover in the Wace Collection illustrated in Burlington Fine Arts Club Catalogue, 1914, no. 72, ascribed to Anaphi. Both pieces were bought by Dawkins in Athens. 53.5 × 34 cm. Dawkins Collection. T.79-1950*

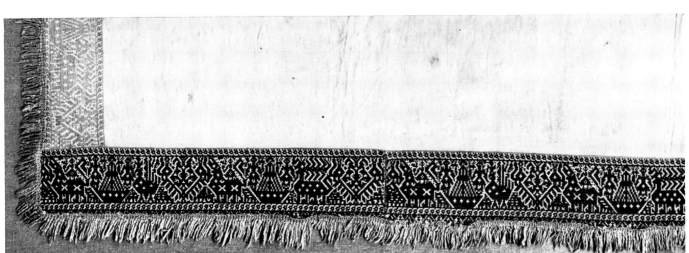

70. *Part of a bed valance. Cyclades,*
Ios. Silk on linen, satin stitch. Red, blue,
green, two shades yellow, pink. Silk
fringe, blue, green and red. 221 × 53 cm.
Dawkins Collection. T.286-1950

71. *Part of a bed valance. Cyclades.*
The original valance yellow silk on linen,
lower border, which has been added, red
silk on cotton. The fringe is also a later
addition. 196 × 78 cm.
Dawkins Collection. T.650-1950

72. *Part of a curtain. Cyclades. Silk on*
linen, cross and long-armed cross stitches,
the seams joined with an insertion
stitch. Blue, green, fawn, pink, yellow.
172 × 151 cm.
Dawkins Collection. T. 462-1950

73. Fragments of a curtain. Cyclades, ? Mykonos. White linen thread on linen. Cut and drawn work with needlepoint insertions, satin and stem stitches. Another fragment of the same piece is in the Wace Collection (City of Liverpool Museums 56.210.119) and was attributed by him to Mykonos. 89 × 71 cm. Dawkins Collection. T.402-1950

74. Detail from a curtain. Island unknown. Silk on linen, darning and double running stitches. Red, blue, green and yellow, outlined in black. Curtains of this type have been attributed to Kalymnos and Kimolos (see p. 20). 147 × 188 cm. Dawkins Collection. T.687-1950

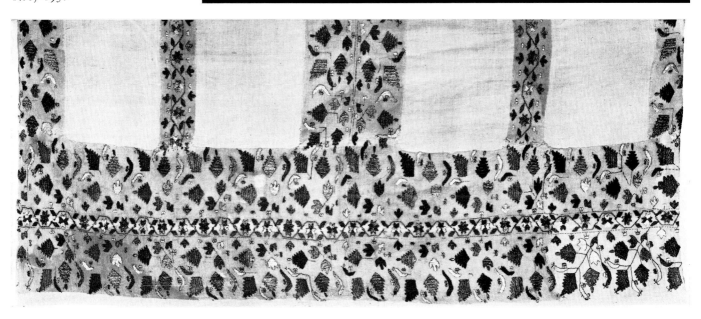

75. *Detail from a bed valance.* ? *Cyclades or Ionian islands. White linen thread on cotton. Drawn thread work, the edge finished with a plaited fringe. The embroidery patterns and style of the valance suggest the Cyclades, but it is not certain that white valances were only made there.* 223×56 cm. *Dawkins Collection.* T.501-1950

76. *Detail from a bed valance.* ? *Cyclades or Ionian Islands. White linen thread on linen and cotton. Drawn thread work, trimmed with white cotton tassels.* 217×49 cm. *Dawkins Collection.* T.473-1950

77. Detail from a border. Cyclades or Ionian islands. Red silk on linen, two-sided Italian cross stitch. Borders of this type found in the Cyclades and Ionian Islands are copied from Italian sixteenth century embroideries. 202 × 26 cm.   Dawkins Collection. T.465A-1950

78. Detail from a border. Cyclades. Green silk on linen, cross, long-armed cross and satin stitches. See fig. 77. 104 × 29 cm.   470-1906

79. *Detail from a bedspread. Northern*
Sporades, Skyros. Silk on linen,
double darning, satin, chain, brick and
double running stitches. Shades of red,
blue, green, pink, yellow and brown. The
edge of the original spread was finished
with buttonhole stitch and a line of
running stitch. The silk fringe is a later
addition. The excellent workmanship in
this piece may indicate an early date.
156.5 × 76.5 cm.
Given by Mrs Bateson. T.57-1926

80. *Detail from a bedspread. Northern*
Sporades, Skyros. Silk on linen, double
darning, brick, satin, back and chain
stitches. The seams joined with an
insertion stitch. Edge finished with
buttonholing and a line of running
stitch. Shades of red, blue, magenta,
green, pink, yellow, brown and black.
Two widths of a bedspread of this type
were bought by Dawkins in Skyros in
1905. 190 × 125 cm.
Wace Collection. T.730-1919

81. *Fragment of a bedspread. Northern Sporades, Skyros. Silk on linen, darning and stem stitches. Red, blue, yellow, cream and brown. 137 × 42 cm. Dawkins Collection.* T.100-1950

82. *Detail of cushion cover. Northern Sporades, Skyros. Silk on linen, double darning, satin and double running stitches. Blue, green, salmon pink, two shades yellow, white, brown and black. 91 × 38 cm. Dawkins Collection.* T.64-1950

83. *Cushion cover. Northern Sporades, Skyros. Silk on cotton, double darning, satin and double running stitches. Two shades red, blue, green, yellow, salmon pink, white and brown. The creature shown here occurs frequently on Skyros cushion covers. It may be intended to represent the Lion of St Mark.*
35.5 × 35 cm.
Wace Collection. T.695-1919

84. *Detail from a scarf. Northern Sporades, Skyros. Silk and metal thread on silk, double darning, chain, brick, satin and double running stitches. Shades of red, blue, green, yellow, pink, white and black. The edge finished with buttonholing and a line of running stitch. Silk fringe and tassels.*
104.5 × 44.5 cm.   Dawkins Collection.
T.49-1950

85. *Border of a cushion cover. Northern Sporades, Skyros. Silk on linen and cotton, darning stitch. Red and green. 51 × 40.5 cm. Dawkins Collection. T.192-1950*

86. *Border of a cushion cover. ? Northern Sporades, Skyros. Silk on linen and cotton, darning stitch. Red, green and magenta. 56 × 41 cm.*
Dawkins Collection. T.357-1950

87. *Border of a cushion cover. ? Northern Sporades, Skyros. Silk on linen and cotton, cross stitch. Magenta, green, blue and cream. The sides joined with an insertion stitch and trimmed at the lower edge with three silk tassels. 53 × 45 cm. Dawkins Collection. T.678-1919*

88. Detail from a cushion cover. Thasos. Silk on cotton, darning stitch. Red, green, blue, yellow and cream. 89 × 44 cm.   Dawkins Collection. T.412-1950

89. *Part of a kerchief. Chios. Silk and metal thread on cotton, cross, satin, double running and buttonhole stitches and drawn thread work. Orange, black, yellow, two shades blue, green and mauve. A similar kerchief is attributed by Argenti to the village of Voreiochora. 48 × 50 cm.*
Dawkins Collection. T.378-1950

90. *Kerchief. Chios. Pastel silks and metal thread on red silk. Cross, satin and split stitches. A similar kerchief is attributed by Argenti to the village of Kampos. 43 × 43 cm.*
597-1894

81

91. *Border (probably part of a curtain). ? Mytilini. White silk on cotton, satin and four-sided stitches and hem-stitching. 84 × 43.5 cm. Dawkins Collection. T.337-1950*

92. *Border of a towel or scarf. Mytilini. Silk on linen and silk, satin, single faggot, cross and double running stitches and woven hem-stitching. White, red, blue, lime green and pink. Fringe of twisted warp threads with red silk tassels. This piece was described as 'made in the island of Mytilini' when it was bought by the Museum in 1879. 112 × 41 cm. 38-1879*

93. *Border. ? Mytilini. Silk on linen, darning, double-darning, fishbone, outline and chain stitches. Possibly the border of a curtain. The silk fringe and plaited cord at the top are later additions. 149 × 17.5 cm. Dawkins Collection. T.326-1950*

82

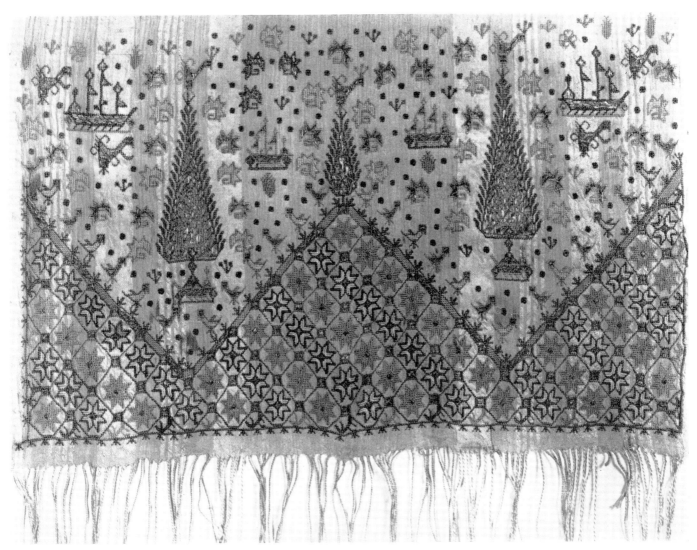

94. *Border of a scarf or towel. Island unknown (p. 22). Silk and metal thread on linen and silk, Italian two-sided cross and satin stitches. Pastel shades of pink, blue, green and cream.* 130 × 41.5 *cm.* T.61-1916

95. *Border of a towel. Island unknown (p. 22). Silk on linen, two-sided Italian cross and satin stitches. Red, blue, green, black, pink, white, some metal thread.* 37 × 41 *cm. Wace Collection.* T.687-1919

96. *Detail from a bedspread. Epirus. Silk on linen, darning and chain stitches. Red, blue, green, yellow and cream. The seams joined by an insertion of bobbin lace. Linen fringe. 259 × 166 cm. Dawkins Collection.* T.249-1950

97. *Detail from a bedspread. Epirus.*
Silk and metal thread on linen, split,
cross and double running stitches. Red,
two shades blue, lime green, yellow and
white. 271 × 191 cm.
Dawkins Collection. T.245-1950

98. *Fragment (? of a cushion cover).*
Epirus. Silk on linen, darning, satin and
outline stitches. Two shades red, blue,
green, buff, white and black. The
figure of a woman is probably intended
to represent a bride. 54 × 40 cm.
Wace Collection. T.692-1919

99. *Part of a border. ? Epirus. Silk on*
linen, darning and chain stitches. Red,
purple, lime green, yellow, two shades
cream. This piece is no. 495 in the
Dawkins manuscript catalogue, where he
says 'Jannina(!) from Paros' – this
presumably being the description of the
dealer from whom he bought it. In the
Burlington Fine Arts Club 1914
exhibition it was also attributed to Paros
(no. 122). 259 × 19 cm.
Dawkins Collection. T.431-1950

100. Detail from a curtain. ? Epirus. Silk on linen, darning and chain stitches. Blue, green, red and cream. The arrangement of the pattern in squares is unusual. The darning technique compares to fig. 99. 249 × 96 cm.   Bequest of Mrs H. M. Richardson.   T.24-1951

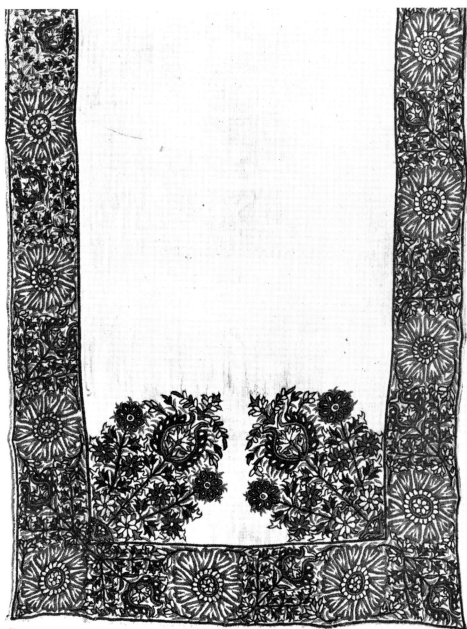

101. *Part of a bedspread border. Epirus (Joannina). Silk on linen, herringbone, chain and stem stitches. Red, blue, green, fawn and white. Black outlining round some parts of the pattern is largely worn away. 103 × 33 cm. 263-1896.*

102. *Detail from a long cushion cover. Epirus (Joannina). Silk on linen, herringbone, chain and outline stitches. Blue, green, red, yellow, fawn and black. 119 × 49.5 cm. 473-1877*

87

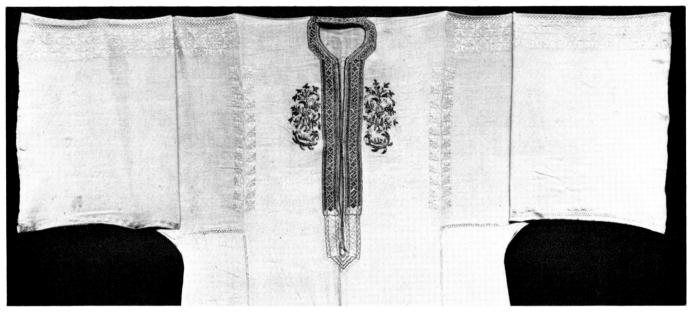

103. *Detail of an under-dress or shift. Epirus. Silk and metal thread on linen. On the sleeves satin stitch, pulled work and hem-stitching, with an insertion of bobbin lace on the shoulder seams. Other seams joined with an insertion stitch. The neck opening worked with metal thread in satin, chain, hem-stitching and buttonhole stitches. The dress has a border round the hem in cross stitch in red, blue, green and black, trimmed at the edge with a black braid. The workmanship throughout is particularly fine. Length 131 cm. Width across sleeves 168 cm. Dawkins Collection. T.339-1950*

104. *Detail from a bedspread. Epirus. Silk on linen, darning and outline stitches. Shades of plum, magenta and pink, blue, green, yellow, two shades of buff, white. Outlining in black is worn away in many places. 217 × 183 cm. T.24-1928*

105. Part of a bedspread border. Ionian Islands. Silk on linen, cross stitch. Red, blue, green, black and cream. Linen fringe. 200 × 78 cm. T.133-1927

106. Detail from a bedspread border. Ionian Islands. Silk on linen, cross stitch. Red, blue, green, yellow and cream. Linen fringe. Acquired in Cephalonia. 217 × 171 cm. Dawkins Collection. T.237-1950

107. Part of a border. Ionian Islands. Red silk on linen, cross, long-armed cross and double running stitches. The two borders, joined horizontally, may have been dress borders. Silk tassels are later additions. 85 × 12 cm. 492-1877

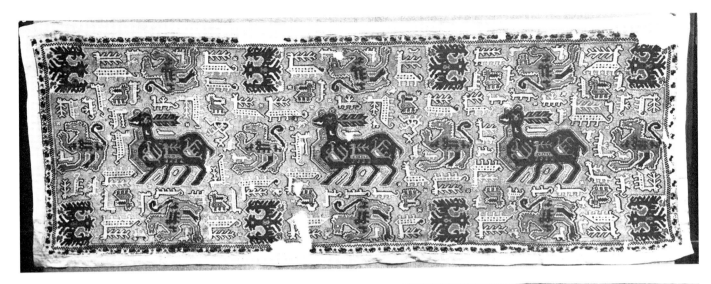

108. *Long cushion cover. Ionian Islands. Silk on linen, drawn thread work, cross and split stitches. Red, blue, green, yellow and brown. 137 × 47 cm.*
Dawkins Collection. T.195-1950

109. *Long cushion cover. Ionian Islands. Silk on linen, drawn thread work, stem, split and whipped stitches. Red, blue, green, yellow, brown and white. 153 × 47 cm.*
Dawkins Collection. T.198-1950

110. Cushion cover. Ionian Islands. Silk and metal thread on linen, drawn thread work, darning, satin and chain stitches. Red, blue, green and cream. 54.5 × 49.5 cm. Dawkins Collection. T.208-1950

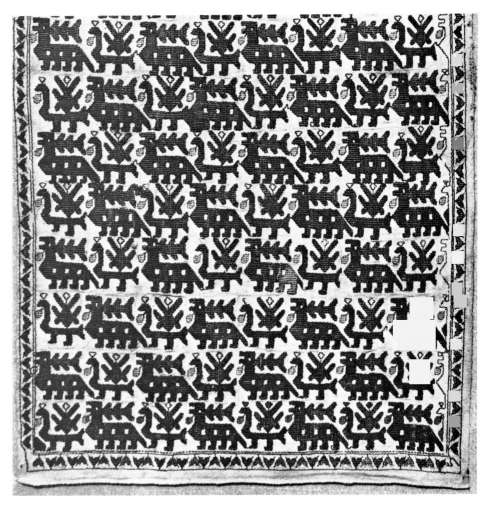

111. Detail from a long cushion cover. Ionian Islands. Silk on linen, cross and double running stitches. Red, blue, green, yellow and black. 116 × 41 cm. 475-1877

112. Detail from a long cushion cover. Ionian Islands. Silk on linen, gobelin and double running stitches. Red, blue, green, yellow and black. 140 × 40.5 cm. Dawkins Collection. T.197-1950

113. *Cushion cover. Ionian Islands,
Corfu. Silk on linen and cotton, cross
stitch. Red, magenta, green, blue, orange
and black. There is a border of small
flowers on the underface. The two faces
joined by an insertion of bobbin lace.
Trimmed with three coloured silk
tassels. 51 × 51.5 cm.
Dawkins Collection. T.356-1950*

114. *Cushion cover. Ionian Islands,
Corfu. Silk on linen, cross stitch. Red,
blue, green, yellow and black. There is a
border of small flowerets on the under
face. The two faces joined with an
insertion of bobbin lace in red and blue.
Trimmed with coloured silk tassels.
50 × 46 cm. 1062-1901*

115. Sleeve of an under-dress. Ionian Islands. Silk on linen, cross and double running stitches and drawn thread work Red, blue, green, yellow and black. Underarm and shoulder seams joined by an insertion of bobbin lace. Length 48 cm. Dawkin Collection. T.338-1950

116. Three dress borders. Ionian Islands. (a) Silk on linen, cross stitch. Red, blue, green and yellow. 54 × 7.5 cm. (b) Silk on linen and cotton, cross stitch. Red, blue, green, black and pink. 69 × 4.5 cm. (c) Silk on linen and cotton, cross and back stitches. Red, blue, green, yellow and black. 59 × 7 cm. 510P.B.J.-1877

119. *Under-dress. Trikeri, Mount
Pelion. Silk and metal thread on linen,
woven with two warp stripes in silk at
each selvage. Cross, satin, double
running and darning stitches. Red, blue
two shades green, pink, salmon and
black. The seams joined with insertion
stitches in different colours. Neck,
sleeves and hem trimmed with coloured
bibila lace. Length 133 cm. Width
across sleeves 153 cm.
Wace Collection.* T.713-1919

120. *Part of a dress border. Trikeri,
Mount Pelion. Silk on linen, satin and
cross stitches. Red, green, pink, brown,
yellow, orange, blue and mauve.
Length 213 cm. Width 19 cm.
Dawkins Collection.* T.340-1950

98

121. Detail from a skirt border. Crete. Silk on linen and cotton, Cretan feather, satin, chain, herringbone and stem stitches. Red, blue, green, yellow, brown, fawn and white. The hem faced to the underside with the same material. 200 × 51 cm.
Sandwith Collection. 2052-1876

122. Detail from a skirt. Crete. Silk on linen and cotton, Cretan feather, satin, chain, herringbone, stem and whipped stem stitches and French knots. Red, blue, green, yellow, fawn and white. The hem faced to the underside with the same material. Length of skirt 109 cm. Width round hem 282 cm.   488-1903

127. *Skirt. Crete. Blue silk on linen and cotton. Cretan feather, fishbone, satin, chain, double running, stem and whipped stem stitches and French knots. The skirt is composed of five loom widths gathered on to a band. Original shoulder straps, adjustable by a cord threaded through two loops. The hem of the skirt faced to the underside with the same material. Two tucks have been made in the length of the skirt above the embroidery. Dated and signed: 1757 Maria Papadopoula. Length 95 cm. Width round hem 348 cm. Sandwith Collection, given by Miss P. Boys-Smith.* T.97-1967

128. *Skirt. Crete. (The two parts which make up this skirt have now been separated.) Lower border, silk on linen and cotton, long-armed cross stitch. Two shades of red, some green. Five loom widths, bound and faced to the under- side of the hem with dark blue cotton. Length 47.5 cm. Width round hem 328 cm. The upper part embroidered in white silk on linen and cotton, cut work and satin stitch. The construction of the upper part at the top is typical of Cretan skirts, and it seems likely that the joining of the two parts was made while the skirt was still in use. Sandwith Collection. 2063 &* A-1876

129. Part of a skirt border. Crete. Silk on linen and cotton, double running and double darning stitches. Red, blue, green, yellow and black. The hem bound and faced to the underside with red cotton. 129 × 43.5 cm. (See also front cover.)
Sandwith Collection. 2049-1876.

130. Two fragments joined. Crete. Silk on linen, darning stitch, the sides finished with buttonhole. Two shades of red. The piece has been cut across the centre in a pattern of scallops and later remounted. 62.5 × 27.5 cm.   Dawkins Collection. T.636-1950

103

131. Under-dress. Crete. The body of the dress consists of five loom widths of linen and cotton gathered to a round neckline. The hem and lower part of the seams trimmed with bobbin lace over-embroidered in coloured silk. Wide and exceptionally long sleeves also fall from gathers at the neckline. Sleeves embroidered in silk and metal thread, Cretan feather, double running and outline stitches. Red, blue, green, yellow, orange and pink. The sleeves trimmed with bobbin lace in metal thread. Length 118 cm. Width across sleeves 171 cm. Sandwith Collection. 2064-1876

132. *Detail of fig. 131.*

133. *Detail from a skirt border. Crete. Silk and metal thread on linen, double darning, fishbone, chain and satin stitches. Pastel shades of pink, orange, green, blue, cream, etc. The skirt consists of five loom widths of linen. The hem and the centre front seam reinforced with a pink silk binding and a dark blue plaited braid. The hem faced to the underside with yellow silk. Length 104 cm. Width round hem 274 cm. Sandwith Collection. 2034-1876*

134. Women's trousers. Crete. The trousers are made of linen and silk woven with groups of silk warp stripes and cut in the Turkish manner with a very wide gusset. Four slits in the waistband, overcast in silk and finished with small insertions of bobbin lace, allow the passage of a drawstring. Embroidered in silk and metal threads, chain stitch. Metal thread worked on a foundation of herringbone stitch. Pastel shades of blue, mauve, pink, fawn and green, with dark brown. The ankles finished with black braid and a tassel. Length outside leg 91.5 cm. 456-1877

137. *Cushion cover. Crete. Silk on linen and cotton, Cretan feather, fishbone, satin and stem stitches with French knots. Red, blue, green, yellow, cream, white and black. The ends trimmed with coloured tassels. 46.5 × 36.5 cm.   Sandwith Collection. 2038-1876*

138. *Detail from a cushion cover. Crete. Silk on linen and cotton, Cretan feather, fishbone, chain, double chain, satin, stem and whipped stem stitches. Red, two shades blue, green, two shades yellow, fawn. 111 × 59 cm.   Dawkins Collection. T.603-1950*

139. *Cloth. Crete. Silk and metal threads on linen, double darning, stem, tent, chain and cross stitches and pulled work. Pastel shades of pink, green, blue and cream. 49.5 × 80 cm. Sandwith Collection. 2029-1876*

140. *Detail from a bedspread. Cyprus. Red silk on linen, long-armed cross, two-sided Italian cross, double running and satin stitches. The edge trimmed with a fringe of white linen and red silk. Acquired in the village of Levkara. 255 × 212 cm.   T.153-1929*

141. *Detail from a bedspread. Cyprus. White cotton on cotton. Insertions and border of cut work with needlepoint lace fillings, satin and eyelet stitches and hem-stitching. The edge trimmed with fringed bobbin lace. Acquired in the village of Levkara. 211 × 161 cm.   T.154-1929*

110

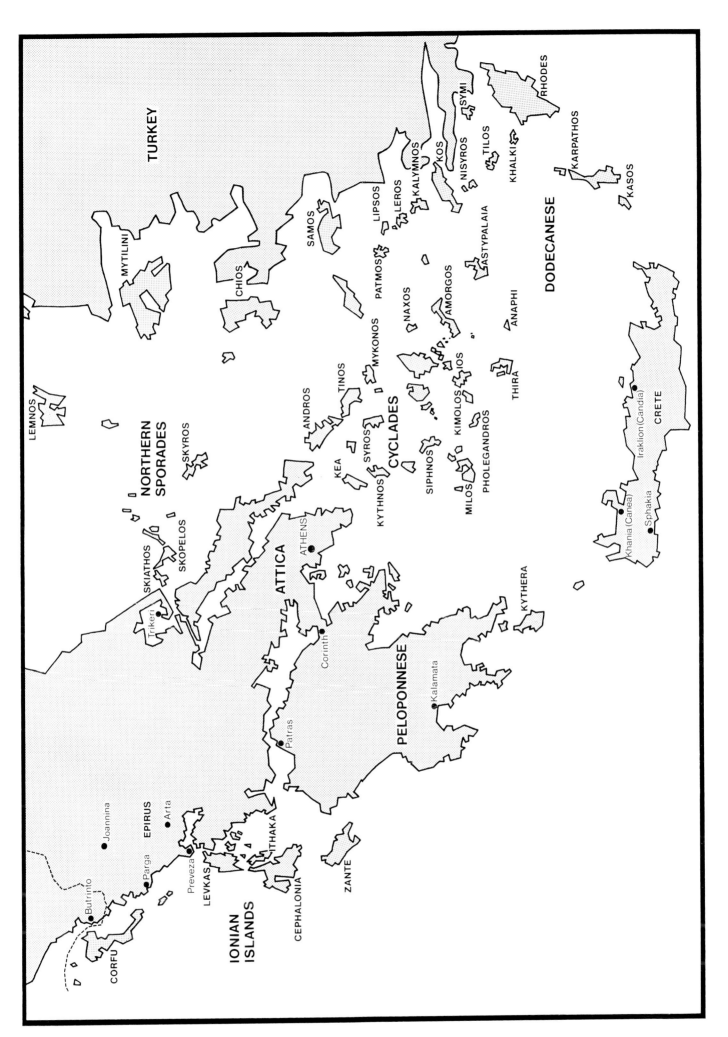

III